HOW TO SURVIVE THE GREAT RECESSION

HOW TO SURVIVE THE GREAT RECESSION

The Resilient Response

Dr Ed Deevy
and Contributors

The Liffey Press

≋the
**liffey
press**

Published by
The Liffey Press
Ashbrook House, 10 Main Street
Raheny, Dublin 5, Ireland
www.theliffeypress.com

© 2009 Ed Deevy

A catalogue record of this book is
available from the British Library.

ISBN 978-1-905785-72-8

Printed in the United Kingdom by Athenaeum Press.

Contents

This book is dedicated to the memory of my sister, Rita. Known affectionately to the Middleton, County Cork community as Sister Regina, her four decades of service as a Public Health nurse left an extraordinary legacy. She'll long be remembered in East Cork.

Preface

THIS BOOK PROVIDES THE blueprint for a positive response to the worldwide economic crash that threatens the psychological and economic welfare of millions of citizens.

Over a period of several months I had become increasingly aware of how the daily drumbeat of bad economic news was having a depressing effect on people. In early April 2009 I was invited by the manager of a small engineering lab in Detroit to come and do some teambuilding. I was not exactly looking forward to the trip as Detroit is one of the cities most devastated by the recession in the US.

Over dinner, on the evening of arrival, the wife of the manager told me that her husband was having sleepless nights as a result of having to downsize his operation. 'He's pacing the kitchen floor at three o'clock in the morning because he has had to let several valued employees go and he's had to put everyone on short time.'

What I discovered the next day is that this manager, Loren Isley, had been able to maintain good morale among his employees despite the recession-related challenges of his business. Isley is that unique type of manager who can 'rally the troops', even in the most difficult of circumstances.

It was a series of experiences such as the Detroit visit that led to the writing of this book. There were no ambitions to write a lucrative best-seller. My belief is that we've had an overdose of negativity since the onset of the recession and that we need to start thinking about the future in more positive terms. This book is about turning the difficult challenges of the recession into opportunities. It is based on my core belief that people can be extraordinarily resilient when facing these tough challenges.

I've drawn on the insights of family, friends and colleagues in writing this book. I especially appreciate the encouragement provided by Jean and Michael Roberts of Sligo. And I'm grateful to those individuals who contributed the insights that are included as sidebars throughout the book. Each provides a unique perspective on how people in different situations can respond positively to this recession.

My thanks to Deborah Dooley and her husband Bob, owners of the *Writers Retreat* in Sheepwash, Devon, England. They provided a tranquil, supportive and stimulating environment to complete work on the manuscript. A word of gratitude also to Kate Gilligan, my former colleague in Massachusetts, for reading the completed manuscript and providing valuable editorial comments.

Finally, I feel extremely fortunate to have found an Irish publisher who could get this timely book to the market with 'lightning speed'. A very big thank you to David Givens of The Liffey Press for his efforts in making this book possible.

Edward Deevy
September 2009

'Difficult times in the world ... difficult times in Ireland.
There is a very special spirit in this country.
It is a spirit that won't easily be broken.'

Bono, U2 Concert, Croke Park, Dublin
27 July 2009

Introduction

WHAT WE'RE EXPERIENCING right now is no ordinary reces- sion. Distinguished Nobel-prize winning economist Paul Krugman says this recession will be with us for three to five years. At this stage we have a good idea of the scope of the fi- nancial crisis that has been brought upon us by greedy bankers and their political collaborators. It's without doubt the worst financial disaster since the 'crash' of the 1930s. It would be im- possible at this time to calculate the amount of human suffering that has resulted from what has been happening. Today, more and more businesses are going bust, houses are being repos- sessed and relationships are coming under increasing pressure. And in this recession, as in the Great Depression, it's the young and low-income people who are suffering the most.

I originally toyed with the idea of referring to the current situation as 'the Mother of all Recessions'. However that didn't put the recession in proper historical perspective. In using the words 'Great Recession' I clearly wanted to rank it up there with the Great Depression of the 1930s that wrecked the economic lives of millions more than 70 years ago. There is a close similarity between these two financial crashes as both were primarily triggered by greedy financial speculators.

As I travel back and forth between Europe and the United States I hear the same story from individuals on both sides of the Atlantic. Put simply, people are scared. They're worried. Even people with relatively 'safe' jobs are becoming anxious about their economic situation.

This book is about how individuals, families and organisations can respond resiliently to the difficult challenges confronting them during this period of economic turmoil. It offers commonsense strategies for coping with this Great Recession. In formulating practical guidelines I've drawn from three decades of work as a psychologist supporting individuals and organisations. To offer a variety of perspectives, I've invited a select group of people from diverse backgrounds to respond to this question: *What advice would you give on surviving the Great Recession?* The written responses, rich with thought-provoking insights, are provided as sidebars in the following chapters. A description of the contributors can be found at the end of this book.

The 16 guest contributors greatly add to the value of this book. I consider each of the contributors to be a co-author. The 18-year-old granddaughter of my neighbour, Amreen Singh, told me how she was determined to get her university degree despite the recession. Her down-to-earth suggestions to fellow college students are included as a sidebar in Chapter 3. Aileen Doyle and Phyllis Brennan draw from their own lived experiences in advocating that people face up to post-Celtic Tiger realities. Their sobering but encouraging advice can be found as a sidebar in Chapter 1. My neighbour, Paddy O'Brien, through his involvement in the credit union movement, believes joining a local credit union would be one positive way of responding to the financial challenges of the recession. He underscores the relevance of the credit union movement to these recessionary times in a sidebar that's incorporated into Chapter 10.

Mary McVeigh's sidebar in Chapter 12 on the need at this time to communicate positive messages to children is recommended reading for all parents and teachers. Deborah Dooley from Devon in England provides a most interesting prescription for nurturing yourself and dealing with the stress of this recession. Her advice can be found as a sidebar in Chapter 2. Linda Desmond of CARELOCAL provides practical tips for older citizens and they can be found in a sidebar in Chapter 9. Lorna Roe and Gerard Scully from Age Action Ireland also provide advice for older Irish citizens underscoring the need for these citizens to be aware of their benefits. Their suggestions and recommendations can be found in their sidebar in Chapter 6.

Katherine O'Leary, a columnist with the *Irish Farmers Journal*, provides inspirational advice to the farming community in her Chapter 4 sidebar. Recommended reading for every farmer in Ireland and the UK.

Jean Roberts from Sligo, drawing on her own personal experiences, shares her thoughts on making lifestyle changes in a sidebar in Chapter 8. Michael Deevy, Chairperson of the Laois Friends of Special Needs, is a long time advocate on behalf of individuals with disabilities. He believes that, with the impact of the recession on government spending, citizens need to become more involved in supporting local community programs. His views are incorporated as a sidebar in Chapter 8.

Christopher Condren, a heating and plumbing contractor based in London, refers to his own journey of self-discovery in recommending that homeowners use the recession as an impetus to make environmentally-friendly home improvements. His commentary is included as a sidebar in Chapter 5. Massachusetts-based Steve Shea urges business leaders to be open to new opportunities in a sidebar in Chapter 4. Michael Roberts, a student of ancient Celtic life and culture, suggests that we need to rediscover our spiritual values in a sidebar included in Chapter 11.

Evan Greer, a 25-year old folksinger and community organizer from Boston, has a somewhat radical view of what's happening to poor people at this time. His comments, found as a sidebar in Chapter 6, evoke memories of the late Woody Guthrie, a travelling folksinger who championed the cause of the impoverished masses during the Great Depression years.

As the reader will discover, all of the guest contributors, while offering a wide diversity of opinion, reflect the view that we need to move forward with a hopeful attitude despite whatever challenges we face.

A list of recommended online resources is provided at the end of this book. Additionally, there's a selected reading list of recession-related books. You'll also find information on how you can provide feedback on the contents of this book.

This book does not specifically address the greed and corruption that caused the economic recession that's now devastating the lives of millions of people. This subject has received a lot of attention in the media and is addressed in a number of recently published books.

The focus in this book is on how individuals, families and business organisations can respond positively to a crisis they had no part in creating. The basic premise is that you can't change what's going on 'out there', but you can control how you respond. In this book I address the various challenges arising out of this Great Recession, primarily from a psychological perspective.

The goal in writing this book is to offer practical, useable ideas – not a lot of motivational fluff. This book is small enough to tempt people who don't regularly read books. It's a book that you could read during your evening bus or rail commute home from work, if you still have gainful employment. Each chapter is summarised with bullet points. This will make it easy to identify the chapters that are of the most relevance to your situation.

While most of the chapters in this book speak to issues of concern to all who are challenged by this recession, several chapters address the concerns of specific groups. For example, Chapters 6 and 7 provide guidance to individuals who have been made redundant. Chapter 4 focuses on the challenges facing business owners and managers. My hope is that you find in this book suggestions that, whatever your situation, will help you cope with the Great Recession.

When I set out to do the research for this book I was faced with the decision of whether to focus on the impact of the recession in Ireland and the UK, or the impact of the recession in the United States since I've been consulting with organisations on both sides of the Atlantic over the past 25 years. I quickly realised that the issues of major concern to individuals, family and organisations transcend national borders. It seemed to make sense to address these issues from an international perspective.

There are some minor language differences in describing the challenges people face. A *resume* in the United States is referred to as a *CV* in Ireland and the UK. Similarly, your get *laid off* in the US while in Ireland and the UK you are *made redundant*. Since this book is being published in Dublin, I've opted for UK/Irish terminology and spelling.

This guide provides suggestions for tightening your belt and living within the constraints of this down economy. You'll get realistic solutions for making smarter choices and living well in this time of economic turmoil. The pages of this concise book are pregnant with tips on the key challenges that now confront individuals and families, including:

- ❖ Why confronting 'the fear itself' is the first step in surviving this recession

- ❖ What to do about recession-related stress and anxiety

- ❖ How to stay positive in the face of all the bad economic news

- ❖ The secrets of building a recession-proof organisation

- ❖ Why you should be planning for an uncertain future while still working

- ❖ Things you must do immediately if you lose your job

- ❖ How to fight back after losing your job

- ❖ Using the recession to rethink personal priorities

- ❖ The benefits of adopting a more frugal/thrifty lifestyle

- ❖ What to do if the worst happens

- ❖ Why we need to see beyond this Great Recession.

Your feedback is welcome on any of the suggestions provided in this book. Simply go to our blog at www.SurviveGreatRecession. blogspot.com. This blog also provides updated information on the issues explored in this book.

1

You've Nothing to Fear
but Fear Itself

BEHIND THE BARRAGE OF ECONOMIC statistics that we constantly hear, one simple fact emerges: the economy in the United States is in a shambles as are the economies of the UK and Ireland. These are the worst of times.

We're stuck in what is the most severe economic downturn since the 1930s. In the United States newspapers and the auto industry are on life support. The employment picture for even the most well educated Americans – men and women with four-year college degrees or higher – is the worst on record. Poverty and homelessness are increasing. One statistic that stands out in America's recession-stung economy is the unemployment rate for adult men: in April 2009 for the second month in a row it surged ahead of the national average to 9.4 per cent versus 8.9 per cent for all workers. The jobless rate for adult women was 7.1 per cent. Blue collar males in particular are taking a very hard hit in this recession.

There are a whole lot of people who are going to be economically desperate for many years. We already know that children are being harmed in families hammered by job losses, home foreclosures and the myriad stresses that grip families trying to cope with economic reversals. The prospects for young people entering the job market are most depressing.

In Ireland, the situation is equally grim. An *Irish Times* article on 6 August 2009 reported that, according to figures published by the Department of Enterprise, Trade and Employment, more than 200 people were losing their jobs on a daily basis. And they reported that there had been a 142 per cent increase in redundancies over the previous year. A breakdown of the figures showed that the worst-hit sectors of the economy were services, building and civil engineering, and manufacturing. That same day the *Irish Times* had a report on a study by the Irish Farmers Association predicting that over 12,000 farming jobs would be lost as a result of budget cuts by the Irish Government.

On my morning walk in the South Dublin community where I live, I pass an ultra-modern multimillion euro complex that is 90 per cent completed but is now surrounded by a ten foot high security fence. There are numerous projects like this around the country that have been mothballed or abandoned as a result of the financial meltdown. A thriving construction industry has died a sudden death. When I pass the public assistance office for my community on my morning walk I see a queue of people waiting outside that is often the length of a city block.

The economy in the UK is also in a critical condition. The 11 May 2009 edition of *The Guardian* reported that 40,000 university graduates of the class of 2009 would be unable to find work. Clearly, young people in the UK are feeling the brunt of this recession. A report on employment figures for Britain pub-

lished in August 2009 showed half the jobs lost over the previous year were those of youngsters, pushing the UK's youth joblessness rate to the highest in Europe. In that same report, offi-
cial data showed that unemployment in the UK jumped to a 14-
year high of almost 2.5 million – a jobless rate of 7.8 per cent.
But it is not just the loss of jobs that's the problem. On a visit to
North Devon in August 2009 I passed through the town of Oke-
hampton en route from Exeter to the village of Sheepwash. My
friend pointed out all the stores on the main street that had
been boarded-up, including a classic English pub that had survived various recessions for almost 100 years. This kind of economic devastation can be seen all over the UK.

As I write this there's as yet no light at the end of this tunnel.
While there are hints of the beginnings of economic recovery in
a number of countries, including Germany and France, the reality is that jobs are not going to return anytime soon. The headline in the 22 August 2009 edition of the *New York Times* had
this headline: 'World Bankers Suggest Rebound May Be Under
Way.' The article reported that central bankers from around the
world, meeting in Jackson Hole, Wyoming, had expressed growing confidence that the worst of the financial crisis was over and
that a global economic recovery was beginning to take shape.
We should welcome every bit of good economic news, including
this prediction by the bankers, however it's likely that the good
times will return sooner for the financiers who played a major
role in creating the financial crisis than for the 'ordinary people'
suffering from the damage. As the unemployment lines grow
longer the jobs become more difficult to find. The labour market
data from both sides of the Atlantic are unambiguously horrible.

What the unemployment statistics don't communicate is the human suffering that's involved.

The Danger of Becoming Crippled by Worry and Fear

What we're experiencing right now is similar to what was experienced more than 70 years ago during the Great Depression. In the midst of that crash, Franklin Delano Roosevelt took to the inaugural dais in Washington, DC and reminded a nation that 'the only thing we have to fear is fear itself'. President Roosevelt understood the psychological damage caused by a bleak economic environment. His memorable speech delivered during those dark days was a call for a resilient response on the part of his people.

Today, people in all sectors of society are worried and scared. Business owners are having sleepless nights as they struggle to stay afloat. Those that have relatively *safe* jobs are worried that they might end up unemployed. Those that have been made redundant desperately search for the few jobs available. Elderly people are coming out of retirement as their pensions disappear with the stock market crash. We're hearing of people in their seventies and eighties looking for work. Many now have to make radical downward adjustments in lifestyle as they struggle to meet mortgage payments and to avoid bankruptcy.

With the economy in shambles, parents worry about the prospects for their children who are completing school. In short, as economic activity grinds to a halt, there's fear in all sectors of society. And this fear is seriously impacting the lives of individuals and families, whether they live in the United States, the UK or Ireland.

A Comprehensive Strategy for Overcoming Fear

In writing this book on surviving the Great Recession I share the belief of the late President Roosevelt that it's *the fear itself* that poses the biggest challenge. This book might have been entitled *The Psychology of Surviving the Great Recession*. As you read through the following chapters you'll realise that *maintaining a positive attitude* is absolutely essential in coping with this potentially debilitating recession.

In the next chapter I'll offer specific guidance on how to confront that recession-related fear that Roosevelt spoke about. It will be clear to the reader that I believe there are healthier ways of dealing with recession-related stress and worry than popping a pill. I make a direct appeal to the inner coping resources of people who are facing various challenges. Taking my inspiration from Roosevelt, I call for a resilient response.

In the remaining chapters of this book I look at the challenges confronting different groups from a mostly *psychological* perspective. One of my major concerns is the impact of the recession on the self-confidence of people. The pervasive negativity in the media can be soul-destroying and debilitating. In Chapter 3 I'll address the issue of how to remain positive in the face of all the negative economic news.

While we've survived previous recessions, this 'mother of all recessions' has many business owners and managers extremely stressed out as they see business dry up. Every day they worry about whether they will be able to stay afloat. I believe the best hope for these businesses is to mobilise employees and customers as part of their survival strategy. In Chapter 4, drawing on my experience as a management psychologist, I'll offer guidance on how employees and customers can be enlisted in the struggle for survival.

This recession is causing incredible stress for individuals and families as millions face the prospect of long-term unemployment. There's the stress of those who have relatively secure jobs but worry about what might happen in the future. There's the trauma of those made redundant sitting at the kitchen table wondering what to do with the rest of their lives. There's the daunting challenge of those trying to get back into a job market that offers few opportunities for employment. Chapters 5, 6 and 7 offer guidance for those workers dealing with the cruel realities of this economic crash.

While some of the changes that people have to make as a result of this recession may cause hardship, the reality is that we may all benefit from having to rethink our values and priorities. There are reasons to believe that some good can come out of this economic crisis. Chapters 8 and 9 provide suggestions on how to come out of this 'age of austerity' with a better sense of what is really important in life.

Chapter 10 provides general guidelines for individuals confronting the worst of challenges – bankruptcy and foreclosure. Chapter 11 has a checklist of the Do's and Don'ts embedded throughout this book. The last chapter reaffirms the need to stay hopeful in the face of difficult economic challenges.

From this brief overview of the issues covered in the following chapters it should be clear that I have full confidence in the ability of ordinary citizens to effectively cope with the various challenges posed by the Great Recession. People are naturally resilient when confronted by tough challenges.

It's How You Respond to the 'Fear' that Really Matters

A recurring theme throughout this book is that you can't do a thing about what's going on 'out there', but you can control and manage your response. *And much of that response has to be psychological.* In a sense we're all *victims* of an economic meltdown that was caused by greedy bankers and the politicians who failed to provide regulations to protect the public. However, from a pragmatic point of view, *I believe we need to channel our energies in support of our own economic needs.* We have a right to be pissed-off with the individuals who caused this crisis, but we need to focus our energies on looking out for ourselves. I call this enlightened self-interest.

There's little of personal value to be gained by playing the Blame Game. And there's nothing that can be gained by feeling like a victim as a result of the current economic crisis. It's helpful to remember that you're not responsible for the financial crash that's causing pain and hardship for millions of hardworking citizens. My advice: forget about getting revenge on the people who actually got us into this mess. *Direct your energy to your own survival.* What's needed to meet today's economic challenges is a proactive resilient response that draws on inner coping resources. For the religious person this may mean getting in touch with their inner spiritual resources.

It will be clear to the reader that I believe that maintaining a *positive 'yes we can' attitude* in the face of difficult challenges is the key to surviving this recession. However, having a winning attitude is necessary but not sufficient in beating this recession. The prudent management of financial resources is also critically important. This book is not intended to provide specific advice on financial management, but rather to offer basic common-sense strategies that can be used to make the most of diminishing financial resources. It should be noted that there are a growing number of popular financial management books in bookstores for people looking for information on how to manage their finances.

℥ ℥ ℥

Aileen Doyle and Phyllis Brennan:

Learning to Live with
Post-Celtic Tiger Realities

'In the 1980s we both, as young mothers, were challenged by very difficult economic conditions as residents of the Ballymun community in North Dublin. We worked hard and fully appreciated the value of a shilling. We are now professional women working in the same community.

Each day in our work we see the impact of the recession. It's clear that over the past decade a lot of people developed unreasonable expectations. The extravagant, keeping up with the Jones lifestyle of the Celtic Tiger was stressful. We were expected to have a new car, book a holiday abroad, etc., and this made us feel good – but that feeling soon wore off. Now, with the recession in full swing, this has changed and this can be a good thing as we can now focus on what really does make us feel good and what is more a true reflection of our values, like giving more time to our family and friends and knowing what's important in life.

With so many of our friends and neighbours out of work it's no longer cool to be extravagant and to flaunt money. Now it's cool to be economical and get value for money. We are all learning to be more careful with money and to get back in control.

In our professional work we both see individuals who get themselves into serious financial trouble because of excessive spending. This causes all kinds of stress within families. Our advice to people who find themselves in this situation is to get themselves to a MABS office or some other organisation offering counselling services. With some professional help they can develop a plan to deal with their creditors. They will immediately feel good – knowing they have regained control of the situation.

Again, this recession may serve a useful purpose in bringing us all back to reality. We each speak from experience when we say the toughest challenges can bring out the best that is within us.'

(Phyllis Brennan is Money Advisor, Ballymun MABS office, Ballymun, Dublin. Aileen Doyle is Manager, Home Support Services, Ballymun, Dublin.)

ℬ℘   ℬ℘   ℬ℘

In the next chapter I'll continue the discussion of how to most effectively cope with 'the fear itself' with specific guidance on how to manage recession-related worry and anxiety.

Tips for Survival:

❖ During this recession keep the focus on your own psychological and economic needs – not on the financiers and politicians that got us into this mess.

❖ Don't allow yourself to be crippled by fear and anxiety. What's needed is a resilient response that draws on your inner coping resources.

❖ Remember: you're not a victim as long as you are in control of your response to this recession.

2

How to Deal with Recession-related Fear and Worry

A S MENTIONED IN THE PREFACE, on an April 2009 visit to a client company in Detroit the wife of the general manager confided in me that her husband was having sleepless nights. He had been forced to fire several valued employees and had to put everybody else on short time. This is a story I've heard from many other managers since the onset of this recession. I've heard stories of individuals worried to death because of economic forces over which they have no control.

Many companies are having to make difficult decisions as the recession deepens. A 7 May 2009 *New York Times* story entitled 'For Small Employers Shedding and Tears' reports on one small Wisconsin company challenged by the recession:

> In a small, windowless conference room, the nine members of the management team at Ram Tool gathered to consider which employees should be laid off in the company's latest round of cutbacks. They debated each name and weighed issues like seniority and skills. Could they do multiple jobs? What was their attendance record?

> Finally, after three days of discussion, they arrived at a list, and it fell to Shelley Polum, the vice president of administration at this small, family-owned tool-and-die manufacturing company, to inform four workers they were being let go. She put on what her husband called her 'stone-cold face' and walked out onto the shop floor. When it was over, trying to maintain her composure, she rushed back to her office and shut the door quickly. Then she sank to the floor and burst into tears.

The *New York Times* story goes on to describe her encounter with the last employee on her list, an employee who with his wife was caring for several adopted children. The worker erupted at Mrs. Polum, asking how he was supposed to support his family now. We're told Mrs. Polum mumbled an apology, guilt washing over her. Like many owners and managers caught in similar situations, she was hoping that what she was doing would help to keep the company afloat.

This same painful scenario is repeated every day in numerous companies throughout the United States, Ireland and the UK.

It's estimated that more than half of all employees in the private sector work in small and mid-sized companies that are now shedding workers in order to stay afloat. One commentator refers to this shedding of workers as the 'silent cull' because it doesn't get many headlines. These are people who go quietly every Friday evening in handfuls. Many work in small and medium-sized retail businesses. They are the sales girls you encounter every day in shops and stores. Some work for automobile dealerships. Others work in manufacturing. They are faithful employees who work in all kinds of businesses. They quietly join the ranks of the unemployed.

There's No Escaping Recession-related Stress and Worry

But it is not just those losing their jobs that are suffering recession-related anxiety. There's almost no way of escaping feelings of stress and anxiety. It's impacting our everyday lives. Many are experiencing all kinds of stress symptoms and it's clear that anxiety and stress are troubling people everywhere. While some are not suffering significant economic loss they worry that they will or they're simply reacting to pervasive uncertainty.

The anxiety caused by the financial meltdown is pervasive. When the full impact of this recession struck I gradually realised that, despite the fact I was not seriously impacted by the recession, the daily recitation of bad news was having a depressing effect. Anxiety and worry were seeping into my life. My response was to try to tune out the bad news. I limited myself to watching television news reports once or twice a week. But I quickly realised that that didn't help very much. Everywhere I went people were talking about how the recession was affecting their lives.

It's clear that the recession and fears of an uncertain future are having a huge impact on the mental health of millions of citizens. Counsellors say there's more marital conflict, more domestic violence and an increase in substance abuse. Mortgage repayments that are impossible to meet are leading to growing rates of depression. Many marriages are failing because the foundations of the relationship have been rocked by this economic crisis. It's early to measure the recession's psychological consequences but surveys suggest a growing impact. In an American Psychological Association (APA) poll in September 2008, 80 per cent reported the economy's causing significant stress, up from 60 per cent in April 2007. It should be noted that this survey was conducted before the full impact of the recession was experienced.

಄   ಄   ಄

Need Inspiration to Cope with this Recession?

The following is extracted from a letter published in the 22 July 2009 Response column in *the Guardian (UK)*:

'... I am 91 and would like to say that with help, it is possible to survive in your own home, as I am doing. I gave up my car at the age of 89, and rapidly realized that this eroded my independence. Fairly soon I suffered a slight stroke; overnight I had to adjust to the fact that my speech was affected and I had to reeducate myself to explore all avenues of communication.

I found some positives in my situation, including that gem – the Meals on Wheels service – whose helpful and considerate volunteers arrive daily and are an important part of my routine... My next-door neighbours have adopted me and have become an extension of my family, who live fairly far away...

My useful thought for those able-bodied in their 60s and 70s who have a social conscience is that they should search out

*those in their 80s and 90s who would appreciate their care
and friendship.*

*I still value my independence: the joys of being in my own
home, under my own roof, where I can brew tea at 4.00 am
and text and email in the middle of the night if I wish. I know I
have more to think about – such as cleaning, repairs, whether
the milkman has called and which day to put the wheelie bins
out – but I'd rather have my head full of these trivialities than
others, such as when the next cuppa is going to be brought to
me or what's on daytime TV...'*

(Cecily.foster@googlemail.com)

ɛɔ   ɛɔ   ɛɔ

Coping with the Recession a Special Challenge for Men

The recession poses a special challenge for men. Padraig
O'Morain, a counsellor and contributor to the *Irish Times,*
wrote an insightful April 2009 piece on the psychological impact of the recession. He quotes *Mind* (mind.org.uk), a publication of the National Association for Mental Health, in showing
the negative effect of the recession on men's mental health.
Mind warns: 'One in seven men is believed to develop depression within six months of losing their jobs and there is an established link between debt and mental distress.' Clearly, with unemployment rising, we can expect a rise in the number of men
dealing with mental health problems.

As O'Morain points out in his *Irish Times* article, there's no
suggestion that women are facing into the recession with some

great sense of assurance that men don't have. It would appear, however, that men's response to recession anxiety can be more harmful than that of women. As *Mind* points out: 'Men account for 75 per cent of all suicides; men are more likely than women to become alcohol dependent; 95 per cent of the prison population are men.' Because we still see the breadwinner role as a male role, the loss of income or of a job hits men particularly hard.

ଛ   ଛ   ଛ

Men Have Limitations!

Somehow the conversation came around to the recession and my barber agreed with me that men are having a tougher time coping with the recession.

'The women are much better at handling challenging situations,' he said.

And then he told me about an encounter with his wife the previous Saturday morning. It seems his wife was a little dissatisfied with his efficiency in carrying out the chores she wanted accomplished.

'I can only do one thing at a time,' he protested.

'That's right,' she responded. 'The trouble with you men is that you can only do one job at a time!'

ଛ   ଛ   ଛ

Why So Many are Stressed-out by this Recession

The factors contributing to recession anxiety are pretty obvious. Joblessness is a major factor. The involuntary loss of a job is one of the most stressful things that can happen to any individual. And the fear of losing a job can be equally stressful. Whole industries are being wiped out as hundreds of thousands are made redundant. It's not difficult to imagine the stress of elderly people who see their pensions disappear as a result of the stock market crash. Families face the threat of foreclosure as they struggle to meet mortgage payments. In each case the source of the anxiety is *economic insecurity*. There's that feeling of not being in control of one's own economic destiny.

Daniel Gilbert, a professor at Harvard University, says in a 20 May 2009 *New York Times* op ed piece that 'an uncertain future' is the real reason why people are stressed out. He points out that 'most Americans still have more inflation-adjusted dollars than their grandparents had' and 'most Americans still enjoy more luxury than Americans enjoyed a century earlier'. The same statements could be made about people living in Ireland or the UK. Gilbert points out that our recession anxiety comes primarily from not knowing what's going to happen to our economic situation in the future.

The feelings of insecurity are compounded by a constant news diet focusing on the negative. The parade of experts talking about recession on every single news bulletin can make us feel more threatened. We lose our grip on reality and start to fear things we have no control over. We're left with the impression that the worst is still to come. But of course it's not just the media that's causing economic anxiety. Most of us know people who are hurting because of this Great Recession, people who are suffering real economic hardship. The reality is that, for a variety of reasons, millions are seriously worried about their economic situation.

Impact of Recession-related Stress on Mental Health

The detrimental impact of worry on our health is well documented – from depression to heart disease. Nowadays, when people feel they can't cope it's to the medical doctor and to medication that they increasingly turn. In my view, this may not be the best response to recession-related anxiety. I don't wish to diminish the real problems faced by people struggling to cope with economic uncertainty, but they won't be solved by popping a pill or sitting in the doctor's surgery.

For obvious reasons there's an increase in recession-related insomnia – people so worried that they cannot get a good night's sleep. Interestingly, one recent study suggests that in treating insomnia, talk therapy may produce better results than continued use of sleep medications that carry dependency risks. The study was conducted by researchers at Laval University in Quebec, Canada. The researchers claimed that bimonthly individual talk therapy sessions, where patients could address residual issues causing them to lose sleep, were more effective than medications. While I can't vouch for the validity of this research, the results suggest that people having sleepless nights over their financial situation might consider talking about these worries to a friend or a therapist.

A couple of decades ago when you had a problem you shared it, if not with your family then with your closest friends. These days we don't have the social clubs and the supports that they provide that were available in past generations. And many people have to work long hours to make ends meet. Human contact is limited to the workplace, the supermarket and the internet. The supportive family is becoming a thing of the past. All of this means that emotional support is not easily available.

‸ ‸ ‸

Deborah Dooley:

How to Beat the Recession Blues

'When things are difficult, remember they'll almost certainly get easier again. If things are OK at the moment, try not to worry about the future, but enjoy the day. Then get moving. Take action to make your life better, and take some exercise to trigger the release of your body's natural feel-good chemicals called endorphins. It doesn't have to be strenuous – any kind of movement is good.

If you wake up in the morning feeling like you can't face looking at your bank statement – get up and go for a brisk walk. Pick a big bunch of wild flowers and put them in the hallway, where they'll make you smile every time you come in. Ride your bike to work, drop in at the local pool for a few lengths, run up and downstairs ten times. You will feel better for it.

If you and your partner are rowing about money, don't. It's a huge waste of time and energy – energy that you badly need! Instead, make a phone call or write a letter to try to iron out some of the financial problems. Then put on your favourite music, pour two glasses of wine, and put your arms around your partner. Dance together, snuggle and hug until you both feel loved enough to protect you from any eventuality. If you feel like it, give each other a massage. Sometimes people find the release of a massage makes them tearful. Go ahead and cry if you want to – it's a healthy release.

Mix up three cups of strong flour, a teaspoon of yeast, a teaspoon of sugar and a teaspoon of salt with enough tepid water to make a sloppy mix. Leave it overnight, and in the morning divide between two oiled loaf tins and put in the oven. Forty-five minutes later you'll have the grounding presence of homemade bread in your kitchen. Plus the reassuring knowledge that it's healthier and cheaper than bought bread. And next time you have a chicken, boil the carcass up for stock, and make delicious nourishing soup with any leftovers.

Eat well, exercise, be kind to yourself and your family and stay calm and positive. Every night, spend ten minutes sitting quietly, concentrating on your breathing, and telling yourself that everything will be alright.'

(Deborah Dooley is a freelance journalist and owner of the Writers Retreat, Devon, UK.)

Ș   Ș   Ș

Even Farmers Experience Recession-related Stress

The recession is causing people to experience stress in all sectors of society. It was a surprise to find this headline in the 2 June 2009 edition of the *Irish Independent*: 'Stressed Farmers Turn to Advice Line.' I was surprised because I think of farmers as proud, independent and resourceful people who would find it difficult to look for help.

According to the *Irish Independent* article, callers to a southern rural helpline were looking for advice on how to deal with major financial worries, acute anxiety and depression. Many calls were from young men who'd lost their off-farm job and were now relying on diminishing returns from the farm. The stress was putting strain on personal relationships with many callers afraid to disclose the extent of their financial problems to their partners and spouses. The helpline is provided by HSE South, a division of the national Health Services Executive.

Guest contributor Katherine O'Leary has very constructive ideas for farmers facing the challenge of the recession. Her recommendations can be found as a sidebar in Chapter 4.

Managing Your Stress Level

There's a long list of strategies that can be used in managing recession-related stress. I asked the manager in Detroit what he was doing to manage his stress. He explained that during spring and summer he spent weekends working in his garden, producing all kinds of vegetables for family and friends. On weekends during the fall and winter he chopped wood to provide fuel for the family's wood-burning stove. These are excellent strategies but not everyone has a garden or wood-burning stove.

To cope with recession anxiety you need to be in good shape physically and mentally. Taking care of your health is obviously basic. A proper diet and a daily exercise regimen are recommended. This can include walking, jogging, biking and a variety of other stress-releasing exercises. Other stress reduction strategies include yoga, meditation and deep muscle relaxation techniques. Your local library and bookstore have many informative publications that can provide useful information on stress management techniques.

A Recommended Stress Reduction Technique

The economic uncertainty that goes with this Great Recession can tie anyone in knots, despite even the best efforts to keep things in perspective and take control. The stress seeps into the muscles of the body. A stress reduction technique I've used for more than 20 years is called Deep Muscle Relaxation. In the mid-1980s I found in conducting one-day workshops for managers that many complained about the stress they were experiencing. As a response, I redesigned the workshop. During the last 30 minutes of each workshop I would invite participants to lie down or sit, as comfortably as they could, and to close their eyes. Then I'd lead them in the progressive relaxation of all the muscles from head to toe. As they tensed each muscle they would hold the tension for about ten seconds and then would let go of the tension, letting the muscles go limp. This exercise drained the stress out of the various muscles. Later I produced an audio-tape of this exercise to give to workshop participants. I was amazed to find out 20 years later that some of the workshop participants were still using that audio-tape on a regular basis.

You can use a simplified version of this exercise simply by sitting or lying comfortably in a room that is free of distractions and progressively tensing and relaxing muscles, beginning with your feet and working your way up to your shoulders and face. Maintain the tension on each muscle for five to ten seconds. When you get the hang of it you'll feel the stress draining out of the muscles.

The Need for a Proactive Approach to Recession Anxiety

As I've indicated, those hardest hit by this recession are those who feel they've lost control over their own economic destinies. It's particularly important that those who lose their jobs or their businesses involve themselves as much as they can in the life of the family, the house, the garden, in leisure activities – anything that keeps that sense of control over parts of their life going. It's important to pursue activities rather than slumping into depression. I'll provide specific suggestions on how to cope with the trauma of being made redundant in Chapter 6.

While it's clear that I believe in a proactive approach to dealing with recession anxiety that includes taking personal control of your life, I also acknowledge that in some cases outside professional help may be appropriate. Most communities now have agencies that offer people advice in dealing with a personal economic crisis. Sometimes psychological support is needed, especially if feelings of desperation take over. A few sessions with a professional counsellor can help the individual develop a strategy to deal with their situation. In certain cases of extreme stress medical assistance may be appropriate.

It's Advisable to Share Your Worries

Sharing your worries with family and friends is often the best therapy. Talking is highly effective for dealing with 90 per cent of low-level anxieties. My experience is that most people are very willing to provide a listening ear for a friend or family member who is experiencing stress.

Over the past decade we've seen a proliferation of technological tools to facilitate communication. These include mobile phone texting, Facebook, Skype, LiveJournal and Twitter. While all of these technologies enhance our ability to stay in touch with family and friends, they're not a substitute for physical face-to-face contact. When it comes to sharing our worries we need the personal contact. *We need to construct small bridges between ourselves* – not texts, emails or tweets, but face-to-face conversations. There's an old cliché that says that a problem shared is a problem halved. It's true! Again, don't underestimate the value of physical activity when you're worried or stressed-out. A long walk with a friend can be most therapeutic.

In the next chapter I'll offer a strategy for dealing with the recession-related negativity that's now pervasive.

Tips for Survival:

❖ Share your worries with family and/or friends. Make use of a strong social support system.

❖ Don't turn to unhelpful coping patterns such as smoking, excessive drinking or taking drugs.

❖ It is important to eat healthy to keep energy levels up. Poor diet can affect mood and concentration levels.

❖ Work off the stress by a regular daily exercise regimen. This can include biking, jogging, walking or time on the tread-mill. Also, consider other stress reduction techniques such as yoga, meditation or deep muscle relaxation.

❖ Don't ignore a financial problem. If the problem is dealt with as soon as possible, the consequences are far more likely to be manageable. If you're overwhelmed with debt go see a financial adviser. This resource is available at no charge in many communities.

3

Staying Positive

HOW CAN A PERSON STAY positive while being barraged by negative economic news 24/7? How can you feel upbeat and motivated when all you're hearing is doom and gloom from the pundits and the politicians? This chapter provides answers to these questions.

Each day there are new depressing revelations. People are losing their savings in the stock market. Thousands are joining the unemployment lines. Banks are foreclosing on families unable to meet mortgage payments. The list goes on. The drumbeat of bad economic news can be heard on just about every television and radio broadcast. Listening to the revelations of millions of tax-payer-funded bonuses going to the executives at the bailed-out banks doesn't do anything for morale. And we're learning how much the politicians, paid to represent our interests, were enablers of the greed and corruption that got us into this mess. It's all very depressing. We're now hearing about a rising tide of suicides related to economic loss. We're told this recession may become more disastrous than the Great Depression of the 1930s. There's fear throughout the populace. As I indicated in Chapter 2, there's simply no way of escaping the daily dose of negative economic news.

Tune in to the evening news on Irelands' RTE and you'll hear the litany of bad news on every broadcast. You'll find a similar litany on the BBC in the UK and CBS in the United States. And the impact of this negativity on the public is obvious. Not surprisingly, it causes fear and anxiety. But it also *has a potentially debilitating impact on the mindset of individuals.* And it's not just people who've lost their jobs or their homes.

The cumulative impact of negative media coverage of the recession is to demoralise people. All this negative news can be a blow to self-confidence and self-esteem. And consider the impact of all the negative news on young people. One mother told me her twelve-year old son was already worrying about the impact of the recession on his future opportunities. Mary McVeigh, a mother and teacher, addresses this concern in her sidebar in Chapter 12.

Individuals who would ordinarily be resilient in the face of life's challenges begin to think in negative terms. And this negativity is like a contagious disease. It spreads as individuals relate tales of economic disaster. Everybody knows someone who's suffering seriously as a result of the recession. *The constant media drumbeat of negative economic news has a powerful impact on the mindset of individuals.* It destroys hope and confidence. People begin to say to themselves, 'we're all screwed'. The negative self-talk takes over.

How to Counteract Recession-related Negativity

As I write this there's reason to believe that we'll continue to be bombarded by negative economic news for the foreseeable future. And, let's face it, some really like to wallow in the negativity. However, my belief is that we handicap our ability to be successful if we are drowning in a sea of pessimism about the future.

In thinking about how individuals should respond to the tide of negative news I remembered an experience I'd had in Ireland in the early 1980s. I was invited to conduct a week-long self-improvement workshop for a group of low-income single mothers in the Ballymun community in North Dublin. These young women had been relocated to Ballymun's high rise buildings from Dublin's inner city in the late 1960s and early 1970s.

After preliminary discussion with a couple of members of the group it was decided that the focus would be on self-esteem. It quickly became obvious that each of these women in the group had picked up a lot of negative messages from home, school and community during their early years. When I asked members of the group to verbalise what messages they had internalised from those early years they came up with statements such as, 'I'll never amount to anything', 'I'm nobody', 'I'm not intelligent' and 'I'll always be poor'. All agreed this negative self-talk had greatly handicapped their ability to be successful in life. Several described how they had a hard time believing in themselves because they had gotten so much negative input in the home and school when they were children.

During the week members of the group developed positive affirmations to replace each of the negative messages they had internalised during childhood years growing up in Dublin's inner city. Included were such statements as 'I'm an attractive and intelligent person', 'I can accomplish my dreams', and 'I'm a special person'. I asked members of the group to repeat their chosen affirmation silently to themselves several times each day. It was amazing to see the remarkable transformation that took place within individuals in this group in the course of just one week. And they were happy to shake off the negative messages that had handicapped each of them up to that time in their lives. I should add that this group included more than a few remarkable women. The self-affirmations just helped these individuals acknowledge what was a fact.

I use what happened in the Ballymun group to suggest how we can effectively respond to the negative messages we are now internalising as the Great Recession comes to dominate our lives. We need to tell ourselves we will succeed no matter how difficult the current challenges. *My belief is that the ability to succeed in this difficult economic environment is highly dependent on our mindset – the way we view the challenges that confront us.* If we believe that, because of the recession, it's not possible to be successful, then we will not succeed. However, if we believe that the world is full of opportunity, we will find it. We need to drown out those negative messages that we are barraged with each day. We need to associate with people who are resilient and have a positive outlook.

The reality is that some people, as I've indicated earlier, like to dwell on the gloom and doom media stories. They prefer to see the glass as half empty. In doing the research for this book I encountered more than a few who questioned the idea of remaining positive in the face of what's going on 'out there'. I'm suggesting here that we need to avoid people who will only drag us down with their cynicism and pessimism.

ℒ ℒ ℒ

Amreen Singh:

My Advice to Fellow College Students: Hang in There!

'First, let me say that those of us in college at this time are lucky in that we don't have to face the threat of being made redundant that so many are now facing.

As well as money, time is one of our most valuable resources. Studying is time well spent and is a great investment in our future. When the recession ends – and it will end – we will have something valuable to offer society. Of course, surviving in college financially can be a major challenge.

I managed my first year because of my part-time job and my grant. For the individual who can't find work during college it is important to remember that if you don't have money now, you will when you get a professional qualification. Any sacrifice you make now will be worth it in the end.

The best thing to do is to control discretionary expenditure and try to keep back-up money for emergencies or unexpected expenses. It may seem like too much to handle ... and some may give up on college and settle for a job they are not happy with. Look at the advantages of college such as meeting new people, memberships of clubs and societies, government grants, student discounts and a qualification at the end of it all that enables you to get a job doing something you are really interested in.

All it takes is dedication. And, again, remember that any sacrifice you make to stay in college will be well rewarded. This is an opportunity for our generation to show the rest of society how resilient we are in the face of the challenges posed by this recession.'

(Amreen Singh is a second year psychology student at National University of Ireland, Maynooth.)

ʕ෴ʔ   ʕ෴ʔ   ʕ෴ʔ

Yes We Can! Yes We Can!

During the Obama presidential campaign I had the opportunity to attend a large campaign event in Boston, Massachusetts. Over 10,000 people from all kinds of backgrounds gathered in the World Trade Centre. Repeatedly during Obama's speech he was interrupted by the thousands chanting, *'Yes we can! Yes we can!'* This was more than a campaign slogan. It was people from many different backgrounds saying that we could have a better society. We could overcome the current economic difficulties. My point is that a simple affirmation had a transformative impact on the millions who heard Obama speak during his campaign.

In summary, there are many practical things that individuals can do to help cope with the recession. I'll be providing suggestions in the following chapters. Amreen Singh has practical words of advice to fellow college students in her commentary that's included in this chapter. Lorna Roe and Gerard Scully offer valuable advice to older Irish citizens in Chapter 6. Indeed, all the guest contributors have timely advice on coping with the recession. The message here is that *it all begins with having a positive mindset*. This is another way of saying that you can't win with a losing attitude. The ability to beat the recession begins in your head.

In the next chapter I'll move on to focus on a group that's most severely challenged by this recession – business owners.

Tips for Survival:

❖ Use positive affirmations to replace the negative messages repeated every day in the media. Repeat these affirmations to yourself each day.

❖ Remember that you are much more likely to be successful in meeting the challenges of this recession if you have a positive attitude.

❖ Control your intake of bad economic news and don't allow yourself to start obsessing about all the negative stuff.

❖ Associate with individuals who have a positive outlook.

4

How to Make Your Business More Recession-Proof

THIS 'MOTHER OF ALL RECESSIONS' is testing the metal of business owners all over the world. Only the most resilient are likely to survive. Businesses that were highly dependent on bank credit for operating funds are experiencing great difficulty in staying afloat. Some businesses, such as automobile dealerships, have had to resort to radical cost-cutting strategies to survive as sales plunge. Despite the best efforts of business owners and managers, many businesses are becoming casualties of this recession.

On an April 2009 transcontinental flight I sat beside a man who runs a steel mill in upstate New York. He talked about how most of his customers were no longer in a position to buy his products because they couldn't get the requisite bank credit. The situation was causing him sleepless nights as he struggled to stay in business. I hear the same story everywhere I go.

Past success offers no guarantee of survival during this Great Recession. In Ireland, Jackie Lavin and her millionaire partner Bill Cullen are considered one of the most successful business couples in the country. In an April 2009 television interview,

Ms. Lavin admitted that she and her partner have been kept awake at night by worries about the economic climate, just like everyone else. She went on to describe their determination to make the necessary cutbacks in order to survive the recession.

Clearly, these are extremely tough times for business owners and managers. After more than three decades of hands-on experience as a management psychologist, I believe there are a couple of things that business leaders can do that will help a struggling business to survive. I hasten to add that there are no easy fixes for companies that have seen sales of their product or service hit rock bottom as a result of global economic turmoil.

On the positive side, the strategies I'm proposing here don't involve layoffs and they don't require additional funding to implement. They do require management to be open to new ideas.

A Strategy for Increasing the Resilience of a Business Organisation

A July 2009 survey of employees in the United States revealed that only one in three had any confidence that the CEO of their company had what it takes to bring the company through the recession. I suspect that the same holds true for employees in Ireland and the UK. Imagine the impact of this lack of confidence in the leadership on employee morale. What this points up is that management needs to be doing much more to engage rank-and-file workers if they are to overcome the challenges posed by this recession. To use a military metaphor, you can't win a war with demoralised troops.

In 1995 I published a book entitled *Creating the Resilient Organization*. It grew out of my work with both public and private organisations in the United States and in Ireland. The key idea in the book is that resilient organisations *are those that have employees who are deeply committed to the success of the business.*

In my book I describe a process that can be used to *engage* employees in the business. At the most basic level this process involves bringing everyone together and providing honest information on the challenges confronting the business. What happens is that employees, given the opportunity, come up with their own ideas on improving the efficiency and profitability of the business. The willingness to tap into this resource can greatly increase the resiliency of any business organisation in tough economic times. What I discovered is that employees, when they become privy to the real challenges facing a business, are often willing to volunteer sacrifices to ensure business survival.

After the publication of my book I began to use a process called 'future search' as a way of engaging and motivating employees. *I found that bringing together the whole organisation and engaging them in a discussion of future possibilities could have an almost miraculous impact on employee morale and commitment.* It can also provide invaluable information on ways of reducing costs and improving productivity. In one organisation, Hawaiian Airlines, I facilitated large-scale conferences involving hundreds of employees. At the time the airline was emerging from Chapter 11 bankruptcy and morale was at a very low level. The conferences included managers at all levels, pilots, flight attendants, mechanics and support staff. These conferences had the effect of making employees feel that they had a vital role in creating a profitable future for the company. And the employee gatherings had the effect of transforming the performance of the airline. I've used a variation of this process in both for-profit and not-for-profit organisations in Ireland.

ఎం ఎం ఎం

Steve Shea:

Advice to Business Leaders:
Be Open to New Possibilities

'My consulting firm provides market research, primarily for companies in the aerospace, defense and related industries. What I've learned over the past decade is that one needs to be flexible, adaptable and willing to learn in this fast-changing global economy. My survival depends on an ability to predict the emerging opportunities for companies, particularly in the area of technology. For example, right now, I know that companies are actively seeking more energy-related solutions as that seems an emerging area that will truly gain more traction over the next few years for many reasons.

My advice to companies that are challenged by this recession is that they be constantly asking themselves what opportunities are likely to stand up in the future. How are things likely to change, what are the new 'white space' areas of need, and how can my company help reshape what we now have in some new directions?

They need to take their subject matter expertise, logically think about potential new markets and applications, and then be willing 'to sell out of an empty wagon' for a while, even if they don't have a fully defined value proposition. Get out of your office with your ideas, build a presentation, fall on your face a few times but let the marketplace be your teacher as you refine your thinking and possibilities. Nobody's going to shoot you and that's the best way to learn new possibilities and see new connections. Just because the old market for your product disappears doesn't mean that you can't use existing expertise to produce a new product or service for another audience. Again, there needs to be openness to new ways of viewing new customers. Often this kind of change will require learning the language of a new industry.

My belief is that this worldwide economic downturn can bring out the best in all of us. We just need to be constantly asking ourselves what new opportunities are on the horizon. And we need to be willing to take some risks. Creative entrepreneurial organisations will play a major role in bringing us out of this recession.'

(Steve Shea, STS Research Group, Wakefield, Massachusetts.)

ဆ   ဆ   ဆ

Your Employees Can Give Your Organisation a Competitive Advantage

I believe that owners and managers need to return to the idea that employees are potentially the best resource for any organisation in a challenging economic environment. What I've tried to do in my work as an organisational psychologist is to show business leaders how they can get the maximum output from their workers. What's clear to me is that it's not enough to just give people a pat on the back and tell them they're doing a good job. Giving positive reinforcement for outstanding employee performance is necessary but not sufficient.

One of the keys to survival in tough economic times is to have employees act as if they have an *ownership stake* in the business and to see their own survival as tied in to the survival of the business. They may be just hired staff but they need to think of the business as *their* business.

The 9/11 attacks on the Twin Towers in New York had a devastating impact on many businesses in the United States. My response was to publish a workbook entitled *Rally the Troops*. The methodology was based on the 'future search' process that I'd used with client organisations in the late 1990s. It provided a step-by-step process for engaging employees *in the business of the business* as a means of boosting morale and productivity.

In trying to explain the concept of engaging employees *in the business of the business* I use my own experience of growing up on an Irish farm during the tough economic times of the 1940s and 1950s. We survived because every member of our large family contributed to the farm operation. Over the dinner table, in a very informal way, my father would share with us what he was trying to accomplish and what tasks needed to be completed to achieve this goal. We all pitched in because we understood what the business was about and we felt we were working for *our* business. I believe the same psychology of getting people to feel they are working for themselves can work in any organisation.

What I want to underscore is that *the sharing of business information* is what makes people feel they have an ownership stake. In management seminars I use a sports analogy to point out the motivating effect that business information can have on front line staff. Imagine attending a baseball game in New York's Yankee Stadium or attending a football game in Dublin's Croke Park and in each situation there was no scoreboard in sight. Without that vital information about who was winning or losing the spectators would quickly become disinterested. Many employees work in organisations where they are not privy to the *score*. The impact on motivation is obvious.

Traditionally, owners and managers have considered employees simply as *hired help*. Here I'm recommending that they be treated as *stakeholders* in the business. This doesn't require any financial outlay. It requires an enlightened management strategy – an approach somewhat like that practiced by my father in our family business several decades ago.

While the idea of engaging employees *in the business of the business* is a commonsense idea, many owners and managers don't seem to appreciate that their employees are the key to the survival of their business. They don't understand the psychology of making their workers feel like *insiders*. Their approach is based on the old notion that paid staff should not be told business *secrets*. Years ago I was willing, as a teenager, to bust my ass on the family farm because I understood we needed to save the harvest to survive the winter. Understanding the needs of a business is pretty basic to worker motivation.

My experience is that employees who are well informed about the business are much more willing to make sacrifices when necessary. In one company that I consult with the employees agreed to work short-time rather than having any of their co-workers be made redundant. In another client company employees were able to come up with enough cost-saving ideas to prevent a layoff. Employees almost always, if given the opportunity, will come up with some of the best ideas for cutting operating costs and improving customer service.

How Your Customers Can Help You Gain Competitive Advantage

The second strategy that I recommend to owners and managers for improving competitiveness is getting input from their *customers*. While this strategy is invaluable at any time it can give a business the competitive edge during recessionary times. Again, the key is to get the customer to feel they are part of an *extended business family*. In one central Massachusetts engineering company I facilitated a day-long session in which the major customers provided feedback to managers and supervisors on their needs. At the end of the day the customers were talking as if they were partners in the business. They had developed through dialogue an *ownership stake*. I know from experience that input from the customer almost always provides valuable insights on ways of improving the competitiveness of the organisation.

There are many ways of engaging customers and getting their input. While a customer survey can yield useful data, there's no substitute for face-to-face interaction. Management of not-for-profit organisations can also improve performance by getting input from their clients.

With the advent of this recession customers have higher expectations. During the boom years many businesses became very lax in their commitment to customer service. This needs to change. Clearly, the company with a strong commitment to serving the needs of the customer is more likely to survive in these challenging times.

In offering these commonsense strategies I don't mean to suggest that there are any easy answers to the most difficult challenges now confronting many businesses as a result of the toughest economic crisis since the Great Depression of the 1930s. The lack of available bank credit will continue to be a huge problem until the large financial institutions get straightened out. Understandably, despite the best efforts of management and employees, some companies will not be able to survive this recession. Given the current situation, I'm convinced that those companies that do an outstanding job of engaging and motivating their employees stand the best chance of survival.

ॐ   ॐ   ॐ

Katherine O'Leary:

How to Survive the Great Recession: Advice for the Farming Community

'The target for farmers is to get through this recession with our businesses intact. To do this we must keep selling produce. We must protect the direct payments by ensuring that we are

compliant with all EU regulations. We must manage the cash flow.

It is important to write down the income and expenditure for each month and to make sure they balance. If they don't then corrective action must be taken.

- Capital expenditure will have to be suspended.

- Costs will have to be reduced where possible, for example (a) Use soil analysis to see if you could avoid spreading P & K. (b) If the milk price continues @ 20c/litre, can you afford to feed ration to cows?

- Livestock farmers must focus on grass production and management.

- Increase income by maximising output, making sure that the produce from your farm is of top quality.

- Pay attention to Teagasc advice. Attend discussion groups and share problems and solutions.

- Shop around for feed, fertilizer and other inputs and ensure you are getting the best value for your euro.

If these measures do not make the cash flow sheet balance, it is time to talk to the bank before they talk to you. Make sure your credit rating is not damaged. Discuss the problems and renegotiate the loans or overdraft facilities. Make loans interest-only if possible.

Remember too that IFA provide a service to farmers who are in financial difficulty.

Some farmers will suffer through this recession and it is important that neighbours look out for each other. Do not allow yourself to become isolated with your problems.

Farmers have always been resilient and we will survive. Let's be positive and create our own bit of history to pass on to the next generation.'

(Katherine O'Leary is a columnist at the Irish Farmers Journal.)

෨ ෨ ෨

Resources Available for Troubled Small Companies

There are a number of resources available for companies struggling for survival. According to an article in *The Sunday Times* (Irish edition, 26 July 2009), stressed out owners of small businesses on the brink of bankruptcy in Ireland will soon be able to contact a free advice scheme backed by the Money Advice and Budgeting Service (MABS). MABS, which is funded by the Irish Government, already provides advice to individuals in financial trouble and negotiates with creditors on their behalf, but does not act for business owners. After a deluge of inquiries to the organisation from worried business owners – calls doubled in the first three months of 2009 to more than 240 – it sought help from the Leinster Society of Chartered Accountants (LSCA).

The LSCA will run the free advice scheme, to be staffed by volunteer accountants. The newspaper reported that the project, called Chartered Accountants Voluntary Advice (CAVA), had already signed up almost 50 accountants. According to the LSCA, its sister organisations in Ulster and Cork are planning to roll out similar schemes in late 2009.

Besides MABS there are other resources available for struggling companies. The County and City Enterprise Boards (CEBs) provide support for small businesses with 10 employees or less. Their website address is www.enterpriseboards.ie. The Department of Enterprise, Trade and Employment is devoted to growing Ireland's competitiveness and quality employment and may be a useful resource. Check their website – www.entemp.ie. – for additional information.

A Need to Focus on the Future

While things are tough right now for business it's important to keep an eye towards the future. In his sidebar in this chapter, Steve Shea underscores the need for business owners and managers to be open to new opportunities. The key ideas in Katherine's O'Leary's inspirational sidebar, addressed to the farming community, can be applied to any sector of the economy. Every businessperson could take to heart her admonition to 'be positive and create our own bit of history to pass on to the next generation'.

In a conversation with nephew Mick Deevy, owner of Deevy Construction, a small construction firm in Dublin, I asked what his advice would be for small companies like his. 'We have to tighten our belts to get through this rough period,' he said. 'We should try to hold on to our best people. And during this down time we should be increasing our capabilities to meet the needs of clients when we start to pull out of this recession.' His idea is that, even though times are tough, owners and managers should be positioning their companies for future success.

In the following three chapters the focus will be on employees and the challenges they face as a result of this recession. We'll begin in the next chapter with advice for those who still have *safe* jobs.

Tips for Survival:

❖ Share business information with employees. They can play a vital role in recession-proofing your business.

❖ Invite employees to participate in discussions of survival strategies. Keep the focus on future possibilities.

❖ Engage employees in discussions of cost-cutting strategies.

❖ If possible, involve customers in recession-proofing your business. Get their input on ways of improving customer service.

❖ Take advantage of the online resources that are available.

❖ Do not allow yourself to become isolated with your problems.

5

Why You Should Look for Work While Still Working

As this recession continues to have a devastating impact on business and industry companies are having to trim their workforces. Even once stable and reliable positions are no longer stable and reliable. Many jobs that historically were considered safe no longer fall into this category. With this in mind I believe the person who enjoys the relative security of full-time employment should use this security to create their own *safety net* for the future. What follows is a description of the strategies that can be followed in building this safety net.

First, it's important to make appropriate lifestyle adjustments. Even though you have a regular weekly paycheck you may want to consider adapting a more frugal lifestyle. Chapter 9 has a list of recommendations, including the idea of creating an Emergency Fund. This fund would have sufficient money to cover basic living expenses, including mortgage payments and household expenses, for at least three months.

Survival Plan A – Be an Outstanding Contributor to Your Company

In Chapter 2 I referred to a company in Wisconsin where management was continuously wrestling with who to retain and who to let go. This is a process that's going on in the conference rooms of numerous companies on both sides of the Atlantic nowadays. Owners and managers obviously want to keep the people who they believe will be most likely to help them get through the recession. With almost every organisation slashing their payroll the best performers are the ones most likely to survive. For this reason your best strategy as an employee is to make yourself extremely valuable to the organisation. This may include a willingness to make sacrifices or go beyond the strict requirements of your job. The employee who works by the clock or abuses the sick leave policy is not likely to be at the top of the survivor list when the axe falls. Put simply, if you are perceived as providing an invaluable contribution you're more likely to survive the next cut. I call this Survival Plan A.

ଚ୦   ଚ୦   ଚ୦

Christopher Condren:

Use the Recession to Make Environmentally Friendly Home Improvements

'First, I need to state that I did not have to make a significant lifestyle change with the advent of this recession. Years ago I had decided I could get along just fine without most of the "luxuries" that are considered the essential trappings of mod-

ern living. I came to the view we have too much "stuff" cluttering our lives. I'm hoping the recession will motivate people to stop wasting the earth's precious resources.

In many ways this economic recession makes me feel validated in the personal value system I've developed over the years. In the early fifties growing up on my father's farm in Southern Ireland I was sometimes given the responsibility of disposing of household waste. I dumped it in the most convenient ravine so that it was out-of-sight. Even at that early age I had a gut feeling that there was something not right about disposing of waste in this manner. As the years passed, living in London, I've become increasingly concerned about how we treat waste in our society. Of course we have come a long way in environmental consciousness since the fifties.

I'm convinced that some good is going to come out of the current financial crisis. We are more likely to have more consideration for how we use the diminishing resources of the planet. And we can all do small things that make a big difference. I live in a residential area of North London and I travel by bike rather than using my car whenever this is feasible. This is good for the air we breathe and great for cardiovascular health! As a former nurse, I'm all in favour of healthy living.

In my work as a small plumbing and heating contractor I now limit myself to those projects that I know will result in some kind of environmental improvement. And I don't like to get involved in carrying out home repairs that are not needed. Fortunately, some homeowners are discovering they can reduce heating bills while making environmentally friendly improvements. I am currently installing a wood-burning boiler.

Later I will install solar panels. Again, a contribution to saving the earth's resources.

My advice is to use this economic downturn as an opportunity to get away from wasteful living and consider ways you can improve our environment.'

(Christopher Condren is a plumbing and heating contractor in London.)

෨ ෨ ෨

Survival Plan B – Develop Contingency Plans for an Uncertain Future

The reality, of course, is that even outstanding performance may not be enough to avoid becoming redundant. For this reason you should be using your relative financial security to develop contingency plans to deal with the possibility of unemployment. The basic strategies I'm recommending are pretty much the same as for unemployed workers in Chapter 7. The advantage you have over the unemployed person is that you have the luxury of a weekly paycheck. In other words, while you are giving full commitment to your current job you are also using your free time to do some advance planning for a possible career change. In an uncertain economic environment it makes sense to live by the motto of the US Marines – Be prepared!

While you are still a full-time employee you need to develop what I call Survival Plan B. To develop this plan you need to think of yourself as having joined the ranks of the unemployed and facing the question of how to move forward. As you envision yourself in this situation consider the various options that are available to you. Your future planning will be dependent on which of these options you are likely to follow should you be made redundant. Of course, you might make contingency plans to explore a couple of different options simultaneously.

I recommend that you take advantage of your present relatively secure financial position to build a list of contacts of people who might be able to help you find future employment should you be made redundant. There are various ways of building this list while you still have a job. You can meet people through conferences and training sessions. Customers can sometimes be valuable contacts. *Having this kind of support network already organised will be a great resource should you later have to engage in a job search*

You can also use your off-the-job spare time as a wage earner to do advance planning for possible future self-employment. If you consider a future business venture as part of your Survival Plan B you can start the research while you're still employed. On weekends you could participate in workshops on How to Start Your Own Business. If, for example, you were considering purchasing a franchise you could quietly do a lot of the research while still employed. *My point is that if you've already done some groundwork you will be ahead of the game should you be presented with a P45.*

The other self-employment option that an increasing number of people are considering nowadays is operating a home-based business. As I will point out in Chapter 7, this option generally has the advantage of relatively low start-up costs. And you can become your own boss. Christoper Condren, whose guest commentary is included as a sidebar in this chapter, operates a home-based business. He enjoys the freedom to be able to take on whatever projects he deems worthwhile. Similarly, guest contributor Jean Roberts also operates a home-based business. She appreciates the flexibility it gives her to be able to combine her professional work with other important activities, such as gardening. Again, you can do advance research for a home-based business while enjoying the financial security of a regular paycheck.

The first step might be setting up a home office. Preparing a business plan would also be a useful exercise. You might never use this plan but it's nevertheless a good investment of your time. It would be a great head-start for getting a new business off the ground should you suddenly find yourself without a job.

In making these recommendations I'm not suggesting that you short-change your current employer in any way. What I'm suggesting is a multi-faceted strategy that includes a high level of commitment to your current job with the simultaneous development of Survival Plan B strategies to address any future contingencies. As the title of this chapter suggests, you should be looking for work while still working. I label this response to the recession as a form of *enlightened self-interest*. This is another way of saying that in tough times you have to look out for yourself. And you have to be ready 'to hit the ground running' should the worst case scenario unfold.

Tips for Survival:

❖ Establish an Emergency Fund that will support you for at least three months if you are let go from your job.

❖ Execute Survival Plan A to insure that you do not make the cut the next time P45's are handout out. What that means is that you are making a critical contribution to the survival of your company.

❖ Be prepared for all contingencies in the future. Discretely execute Survival Plan B.

6

How to Cope with the Trauma
of Becoming Unemployed

U NEMPLOYMENT RATES ARE at their highest in years and behind every statistic is a human story of disappointment and
fear. Telling somebody who's frightened for their future to focus
on the positive aspects of job loss may sound a bit hollow, but is
there any other choice? In this chapter I'll describe how to make
the best of what clearly can be a most traumatic experience.

Experts on how to beat the job-loss blues advise the newly
unemployed person to use this time to re-think, restart and follow the dream of rebalancing work and home. I'll have more to
say on using the recession as an opportunity to revisit personal
priorities in Chapter 8. Here I want to focus on coping with *the
emotional trauma of getting a P45*. In the next chapter I'll offer
specific recommendations about how the person who has lost
their job can regain economic security. The person who does the
kind of contingency planning described in Chapter 5 will be in a
better position to make a career change or find another job.

In Ireland and the UK we talk about workers becoming *redundant*. In the United States it's more common to talk about
workers getting *laid off*. The reality, whatever language you use,

is that it has become a defining outcome of this Great Recession. More people will get P45's during this recession than at any previous time in history. What we're seeing now are massive layoffs that are sending hundreds of thousands to the dole queues. In Ireland, within just a few months a dynamic construction industry has come to a grinding halt. In the United States, General Motors, at one time the largest automaker in the world, filed for bankruptcy protection in late May 2009. The bankruptcy is certain to lead to major job cuts at the company. What's sometimes overlooked is that Detroit's woes are wounding an army of suppliers. The auto supply companies, many small, family-owned businesses, employ more workers than the car companies themselves. One industry spokesperson predicted that 500 out of 4,000 suppliers will go out of business during the second half of 2009. The layoffs are likely to get worse before the economy recovers.

The current recession is presenting a greater challenge for individuals made redundant than past recessions. In previous recessions when people were made redundant they had the option of relocating to find work. This time there's no place to go. In the 1980s young Irish workers could relocate to Boston or New York. Workers from the rust belt in the Midwest of the United States were able to relocate to the South or Southwest. Now, as millions join the unemployment lines, they are facing the possibility that they may not be able to find new employment anywhere within the foreseeable future.

Memo to Company Management:
There is an Alternative to the P45

Before going on to discuss the trauma of getting a P45, I should
point that there are alternatives in some situations to firing employees. Clearly, companies should only pass out the P45's as a
last resort. Management needs to consider the long-term interests of the organisation before they wield the axe. I know from
experience that it's extremely difficult to regain employee morale
after a major layoff. Recent reports suggest that some companies
are trying other options. An 11 July 2009 article in *The Guardian*
reported that BT and other high-profile firms were offering employees time off in exchange for a wage cut. The article pointed
out that an increasing number of employers are using this approach in order to retain valuable staff in the long term while cutting costs in an effort to survive the recession.

These redundancy avoidance strategies are uncharacteristic
of anything that happened in the 1990s recession. In the past,
companies never thought about the negative effects of mass com-
pulsory redundancies. Now they realise that if you want a happy,
engaged workforce you don't start by dismissing as many people
as you can.

Of course, the offer to take cuts in hours and pay is not ideal
for many, particularly those with families and large mortgages
to pay. But for other employees, who have no children or big
financial commitments, the idea of getting some time off, and
getting some money to do it, has obvious appeal.

How should employees who take up such offers use their
new-found free time? Clearly this time off is an invaluable op-

portunity to boost future career prospects. Some might consider overseas volunteer work with one of the dozens of charities that use skilled volunteers. For those who have been told to take time off, thecareerbreaksite.com has a wealth of information on volunteering overseas and in the UK. Volunteer.ie is the website of the national organisation with responsibility for promoting volunteering in Ireland, both nationally and locally.

Unfortunately, the reality during this recession is that most businesses will choose the P45 over any kind of alternative arrangements.

$$\text{\small{ঙ}\quad\text{\small{ঙ}}\quad\text{\small{ঙ}}}$$

Evan Greer:

Keeping Your Spirits Up during the Recession: A Message to Young People Everywhere

I'm a 25-year old travelling folksinger and community organiser based in Boston. I have seen the effects of this most recent economic recession first-hand as I move from city to city and small towns across the US. I may be young, but I've been travelling long enough to know that this isn't something new. For poor folks and communities of colour, injustice at the hands of a greedy economic system is written into the history of this nation. In my city, Boston, where thousands of Irish immigrants came to seek refuge from Famine-genocide, a new generation of working-class families now face foreclosure and eviction due to gentrification, predatory lending, and Wall Street hooliganism. When you set this to the backdrop of impending en-

vironmental crisis due to climate change (caused by greedy corporations) the recession starts to sound like a great reason to get depressed.

So what to do? We keep our spirits up in the way we know how: music, dance, communal meals and close-knit communities. We can reduce our dependence on corporations and governments with projects as simple as a back yard or rooftop garden. Producing our own food in the city will become more and more necessary as fuel prices increase. Collective living arrangements can provide an economic alternative to nuclear families, reducing waste and costs and allowing for shared childcare and domestic responsibilities. I bike instead of drive, I cook instead of eating out, I borrow and share resources with my neighbours instead of buying new.

Creating alternatives to capitalism and greed is less ideological these days than it is practical, but in times like these, resistance to the system that brought us to this point becomes essential. In Boston, dozens of people have participated in civil disobedience, forming "eviction blockades" to keep families in their homes and to force greedy banks to negotiate. In Oaxaca, Mexico, teachers and indigenous people rose up to demand sovereignty from neoliberal economics that were destroying their communities. Across the world, people are finding power in their communities to create new systems and hold accountable the profiteers who have led us down this frightening path. We all have our role to play in this growing global movement. Mine is to sing songs and remind young people they are not alone, and give them some hope and inspiration for the struggle to come.'

(Evan Greer is a folksinger and community organiser in Boston, Massachusetts.)

ഇ   ഇ   ഇ

The Shock of Becoming Redundant

Being told that you are about to become redundant creates deep emotional responses. Even if you had an inkling that the axe might fall you are still likely to experience shock. If you were deeply invested in your job you are likely to experience a grieving process. Psychologists have likened the situation of the person involuntarily made redundant to the person informed that they have a terminal illness. In each case, the person goes through the stages of grieving beginning with denial and anger and eventually ending with acceptance.

The involuntary loss of a job involves a serious life change. It immediately has an effect on your feelings of financial security. And this can be very scary for an individual who has serious ongoing financial commitments, such as a monthly mortgage payment. The loss of a job also affects your personal status. This is particularly true if your identity is very much tied up with your job and career. Becoming redundant can also have a major impact on your relationship with your spouse or partner. And of course becoming redundant can have a major impact on how you feel about your own competence and expertise.

The person who is suddenly unemployed has serious emotional challenges to deal with. The process of dealing with these intense emotional feelings may take weeks or months. The reality is that getting fired, even if it is due to factors beyond your control, is a painful experience for most people. Suddenly, you find yourself on the sidelines while your upwardly mobile friends and neighbours are still working. Being unemployed in our culture has a certain stigma. There's no easy formula for dealing with the emotions that go with this experience. You just have to live through it.

How Men Cope With Job Loss

In Chapter 2 I referred to the fact that while getting fired can be very stressful for anyone it can be particularly traumatising for men. Because men are traditionally the main earners in the family, and because we often still see the breadwinner role as a male role, the loss of income or of a job hits men particularly hard. And the recession is decimating workers' employment prospects in traditionally male-dominated industries such as construction, finance, the motor trade and retail management. In Ireland, more than two men are joining the dole queues for each woman who signs on for the first time.

Men adjust to redundancy in one of two ways. Older men from a more traditional background can find it terrifying. Younger men who've been part of a more egalitarian relationship, where both parties work and both take care of the housework and children, tend to adjust fairly well.

Aside from the day-to-day challenges of stepping into the domestic sphere, the hardest thing for many men – and indeed women – who have been made redundant is the loss of identity they suffer. Our identity is largely bound up in work. The shock of losing the job is tremendous and that takes a while to recover from. It's a bit easier when it has happened as part of a major structural change in the economy such as the current recession, but it is still a difficult adjustment.

As already mentioned, women are generally better equipped than men to deal with redundancy. A 2005 study carried out by sociologists at the University of Warwick found that most couples – across all social classes – continued to view men as providers, even when the woman had become the breadwinner. 'Losing their jobs wasn't such a problem for women, as they said it was easier to find other things to do, whereas their husbands were, many felt, like spare parts hanging about the home,' the authors said.

Again, what I want to underscore here is the fact that there are some significant differences in the way men and women respond to the experience of losing their job. But it needs to be reaffirmed that the experience is emotionally stressful for both men and women.

ഔ ഔ ഔ

Lorna Roe and Gerald Scully:

Advice to Older Irish Citizens: Be Informed about Your Benefits

'A recent survey in Ireland showed how pensioners could teach us all a lesson on "living within their means". Be it life experience, or possibly life's harsh lessons, older people in Ireland are survivors. However the majority of pensioners in 2007 (most recent data) lived in the bottom three income deciles on

€278 a week or less – a stone's throw from the risk of poverty
line at €228.65 a week. Indeed, 16.6 per cent of all older people
lived in poverty below this amount. However, interestingly, the
consistent poverty rate, the rate of people who say their in-
come affects their ability to buy key goods and services, re-
mains low at 2 per cent.

Here is a key example of perception of need or deprivation.
Deprivation indicators are formed on the basis of both social
deprivation and physical deprivation – social being similar to
Adam Smith's argument that every man should own a pair of
leather shoes and a linen shirt for respect and dignity, and
physical being, for example, the ability to buy food and heat
for one's home. And here lies the crux of the situation.

Age Action Ireland recently had a "food or fuel" campaign
to highlight a decision many pensioners were being forced to
make on a daily basis in the context of rising energy costs. Do
they buy their food or their fuel this week? However, in a sub-
sequent meeting Age Action Ireland had with civil servants on
this topic a very interesting finding came out – not all older
people were using their fuel allowance that came with a benefit
called the Household Benefits Package. It seemed many were
afraid to use the benefit as they didn't know how it worked and
were terrified of running up a bill. As a result, people were
needlessly freezing in their own homes.

Benefits are your safety net. When you work you contribute
a percentage of your salary into the PRSI fund. That fund ex-
ists for you should you experience hardship. The trick is, people
involuntarily pay into the system through a ready-made (and
efficient) collection network but they voluntarily receive from a

system that many would argue is fragmented and difficult to negotiate. The lesson is: get informed and don't be afraid to ask. We know from our research that there are several benefits, including the Household Benefits Package and the Fuel Allowance, that people either don't use properly or don't ask for.

Our advice to older Irish citizens is that, during these difficult recessionary times, they make it their business to educate themselves about their benefits and entitlements.'

(Lorna Roe is Social Policy Officer/Social Partnership and Gerard Scully is Senior Information Officer at Age Action, Ireland.)

ဆ ဆ ဆ

Impact of Redundancy on Couples

Redundancy can cause very difficult adjustments in the lifestyle of couples and families. Couples going through a difficult transition brought on by the loss of a job by either spouse need to appreciate the different values they bring to the household. *If the husband and wife meet the challenges as a team they are more likely to weather the storm.* It's important that they maintain as much normalcy in their lives, including staying in contact with their old social circle. And of course *couples need to constantly talk and share what each is experiencing.*

The loss of a job can lead to money trouble and this can lead to relationship difficulties. The latest figures from Accord, the largest marriage counselling service in Ireland, show that the number of clients citing finances as a problem for their marriage rose from 20 per cent in 2007 to 31 per cent in the first half of 2009. These figures are likely to increase as the recession deepens.

As redundancy hits home for more and more couples, women are increasingly finding themselves thrown into the main breadwinner role – while the men get to spend more time with the children. I believe there's now the possibility to transform the trauma of job loss into new opportunities. In Chapter 8 I'll discuss how the recession, and in particular involuntary job loss, can have the beneficial effect of helping people re-balance their lives.

After a Job Loss You Need to Stay Fully Engaged with Life

Those who are hardest hit in a down economy are those who feel they have lost control over their own lives. As suggested earlier in Chapter 2, *people who lose their jobs or their businesses need to involve themselves as much as they can in other activities such as family, the house, in leisure activities* – anything that keeps that sense of control over parts of their life going. The person who has lost their job needs to stay fully engaged with life.

If you don't have a family it's important to pursue activities rather than slumping into depression. This can be fishing, digging a garden, doing house repairs, walking ten miles a day, creating a blog – anything that keeps you fully engaged with life.

By insisting that there's more to your life than your employment status, by keeping busy in any area of your life in which you have control, you can get through what is an emotionally difficult experience in better shape than if you spend your days in front of a television watching Jerry Springer or Judge Judy. It's not a good idea to become what Americans refer to as a *couch potato*.

Strategies to Help Make the Transition from Employment to Unemployment

There are a number of constructive things you can do that will help as you make the difficult transition from the life of an employed person to that of an unemployed person. Here are a number of suggestions to consider:

- *Don't panic and don't beat up on yourself for having lost your job.* And don't waste your valuable energy blaming the bankers and the politicians who are responsible for this economic disaster. Keep your cool!

- *Don't burn any bridges on the way out.* That person who gave you the P45 may be able to help you in your search for your next job. And sometimes people get called back if the economic situation within the company improves.

- *Find out about your benefits.* Andrew McCann's *Know Your Rights* (Blackwell Publications, 2009) is a guide to entitlements in Ireland and a valuable source of information. The Recommended Online Resources list at the end of this book has several websites that provide useful information. Check to see what health care or unemployment benefits you may be entitled to. I generally recommend that you bargain for a cash payment in lieu of an outplacement counselling service, particularly if you have already used this kind of programme in the past. While some outplacement programmes are helpful you may be better off having the extra cash in your bank account.

- *Take control of your personal and family finances.* Develop a budget and make sure you are conserving your limited resources. Your budget should be based on the assumption that you'll be unemployed for more than a few months. In Chapter 9 I offer specific details on recession-related belt-tightening and other lifestyle changes.

After you've taken immediate steps to insure a soft landing turn your attention to developing a new lifestyle as an unemployed person. For some men, this will involve developing a new role as house-husband. The important thing to remember is that you are now working full-time for yourself and your family – as distinct from working for some corporate entity. You still have a 'job'.

I'll have more specifics on your efforts to re-establish your financial security in the next chapter. In the meantime, here are a few preliminary steps that should be undertaken as quickly as possible after you have been made redundant:

- *Organise your home for 'work'.* Create a space in your home that's conducive to work. It can be difficult to conduct a job search or plan a future business venture from the kitchen table. The local library or a favourite coffee-shop can also be part of your work space.

- *Develop and maintain a daily 'work' schedule.* Don't sit there – act industrious. Dress for 'work'. Sitting around in your pyjamas is not the way to go if you want to get back into the job marketplace. I recommend you start early each day and develop a list of things to do that day.

- *Take control of the housework situation.* If you have taken on the role as house-husband it may be helpful for your wife or partner to develop a 'to do' list for you each day until you get comfortable in your new role. If you are well organised you can balance your household and family responsibilities with the task of planning for the future.

- *Make yourself feel useful.* To get out of the rabbit-hole of negative/fear-based thinking ask, 'What can I do right now that's useful?' I suggest utilising this spare time you have right now to volunteer. Ask yourself, where can I serve? How can I share my unique talents, gifts and experiences to make a difference? I guarantee you that if you can find a way to be of service, even just for a few hours a week, you will stop feeling useless. The website, www.volunteer.ie, has information on volunteering in different parts of Ireland. If you are interested in helping other people trying to cope with the recession you might volunteer a few hours with the Salvation Army, the Samaritans or the St. Vincent de Paul Society. Your local library and other local organisations are increasingly looking to volunteers to supplement the work of staff.

- *Explore in-between opportunities.* It might be a part-time gig a couple of times a week. Don't be afraid to swallow your pride and accept something that is below your level of skill and competence. The therapeutic value of getting out of the house may be more important than the small amount of income involved.

- *Include some enjoyable things in your life.* Take advantage of the freebies. Scan the events guide of your local newspaper. Most communities have lots of stuff free of charge. Socialise at home – it's cheaper. If you have a garden, get busy planting some vegetables. Use your time to develop new skills. Think of the things you always wanted to do but just did not have the time. It is really important to stay busy and fully engaged with life.

- *Don't let your home become a prison.* Get out every day and be happy to see people. As much as possible associate with positive go-getting people and be willing to ask for advice. Spend at least 30 minutes on a workout four or five mornings each week.

Again, I want to underscore how stressful it is at any time to involuntarily lose a job. This stress is compounded in an environment where the possibilities of re-employment are scarce. The practical steps I've outlined in this chapter are intended to make a difficult situation more manageable. The Citizen Information Board offers a website that you may find helpful. The address is www.losingyourjob.ie. It provides information for those currently unemployed or who are becoming unemployed.

In the next chapter I'll offer specific recommendations that can be pursued in the face of possible long-term unemployment.

Tips for Survival:

❖ Understand that job loss involves a serious life change that causes deep emotional responses. It may take time to come to terms with your new unemployment status.

❖ Pursue a variety of activities rather than slumping into a life of depression. Put a priority on regular daily exercise.

❖ Maintain your old social network. Consider inviting friends over occasionally for pot-luck dinners. This will allow you to maintain the contact without incurring a major expense.

❖ Take immediate steps to address your financial situation, including developing a realistic budget.

❖ Develop a daily work schedule that includes household responsibilities as well as forward planning to insure your future financial security.

7

After Redundancy –
The Resilient Response

I N THE LAST CHAPTER I SUGGESTED that your first priority after
you've been made redundant is to regroup and take care of
your immediate financial situation. It's also important to allow
some time for psychological recovery. William Bridges, an
American psychologist who focused his practice on helping
newly divorced people cope with change, stresses *the need to let
go of the past before moving on*. There needs to be a period of
bereavement after becoming unemployed before getting
cranked up to move forward. It may take weeks or even months
before you're psychologically ready to become fully committed
to exploring future opportunities.

Once you are in a positive and realistic mindset, and at
peace with the redundancy decision, you are ready to seize the
future. Your old job is a thing of the past and you must now
think of your future career. Again, you must first get your head
in the right place. Organisations will only want to hire or deal
with those who are achievers *with the right attitude*.

First Analyse Your Situation

Your first task after you have come to terms with your job loss is to analyse your current situation. Ask some basic questions. What do I want right now? Are there possibilities other than a nine to five job? Resist the temptation to jump immediately into a job that might be wrong for you. I've known more than a few people who made that mistake after becoming redundant.

With this recession we're now looking at a remarkable transformation in the employment landscape. As mentioned in Chapter 2, there are hundreds of thousands each week who are victims of the *silent cull*. Those construction jobs in Ireland may not return soon. And those automotive jobs in Detroit may never return. I have friends who work in the auto industry that know that their jobs have disappeared forever. Clearly, many will not be able to find employment in their own field. Many of the jobs lost in the financial sector are not coming back. All of this means that unemployed workers will have to think outside the box if they are to find economic security. The reality is that there may not be another nine to five job with pension and generous benefits at the end of the search.

I suggest that an individual who is made redundant, after spending the necessary time adjusting to their new situation, keep an open mind about future opportunities. Today, employees made redundant need to think about how they can market their skills in a profoundly changed economic environment. It's likely that many will have to make a major career change.

Get Organised/Stay Positive

Let me begin by offering some suggestions to those who are pursuing a traditional job search. The advice I offered in the last chapter about setting up a work environment in your home is critically important. Searching for employment in a tight job market needs to be approached in a well-organised and highly professional manner.

It's easy to succumb to depression when you're looking for a job in a marketplace where there are few to be had. You must stay positive, which means you can't inhale too much of the negativity coming to you from your television screen or your radio dial. I know that a fresh breath of positive thinking is not going to get you a job, but it can certainly help. As pointed out in Chapter 3, you can't win with a losing attitude. Since thought follows action, *one of the best ways to inspire positive thoughts is by doing things in your life that are productive.* That's why when you do something positive towards your goal of finding a job you're likely to feel better.

Build a Support Network

As you get ready to conduct your job search your first consideration should be making sure you have in place a support network. Here are a couple of ideas to consider:

- *Focus on personal contacts.* Your computer will be a valuable tool as you conduct your job search, but it will not provide the personal contacts or support that are an essential part of an effective job search. My advice is to incorporate more of the *human element* instead of using the internet as your primary search tool. Step away from the computer. Make a list of everybody you know as more than just an acquaintance. These are the people who may be able to give you a lead on a job opportunity. Each day spend at least one hour calling the individuals on your list to connect, network and ask for feedback, advice and possible introductions to additional contacts. Start each conversation by catching up and taking a sincere interest in their life – it's important to connect before going into a conversation about your employment situation. Have a script and be courageous and ask the person if they know anyone in any field that would be open to doing an informational interview with you. *Make your intention for each call to grow your list of connections and possibilities.* In addition to the phone calls it may be advisable to send a friendly note to everybody on your contact list letting them know you are *in the market* for a job. Tell your contacts that you'll appreciate all possible leads. The more introverted you are the more difficult this task will be. However, you need to muster up the courage! When you're getting discouraged remind yourself that most unemployed people find jobs as a result of referrals by friends or former colleagues.

- *Consider joining or setting up a support group.* In New York a group of unemployed people have set up what they call the 405 Club, named for New York's maximum unemployment benefit of $405 a week. The group provides a support network for the growing number of jobless in New York. Their goal is to share tips on how to live within their drastically reduced means, offer each other moral support and ultimately help each other find jobs. You might consider setting up a similar group in your community. Even meeting with three or four other unemployed colleagues once a week for an hour in a local coffee shop can provide a valuable sounding board. It can also provide invaluable emotional support.

Tips on Conducting Your Job Search

If you're conducting a job search for the first time as an unemployed person you may want to check out some of the valuable resources that are available in your local bookstore or library. In the meantime, here's a list of recommendations to keep in mind:

- *Get yourself out there into the marketplace.* Physically walk into companies and places of business that interest you and introduce yourself. Ask for an application form and complete it immediately on-site. And be sure to always have an up-to-date copy of your CV with you so that you can hand it in and request to meet the hiring manager directly. Again, conducting your job search exclusively or primarily online is limiting. Don't underestimate the value of face-to-face interaction. You are more than a piece of paper with bullet points.

- *Pick up the phone.* Be sure to get yourself into a real positive frame of mind before you make that call. You don't want to sound desperate. Generally, it's better to make the calls early in the day when you have the most energy.

- *Develop a CV that highlights the specific skills that you can offer a potential employer.* Take the time to customise your cover letter and core CV to the particular position that you are applying for. Of course, this implies that you have done your research and know what your potential employer is looking for. If you're sending your documents by email, be sure to use your name to name the file. This will make it easier for a hiring manager who may be dealing with hundreds of applications.

- *Consider it a victory in today's job marketplace when you score an interview.* With so many competing for so few positions, it is a good sign if you are getting interviews.

Looking for Jobs Online

While the major focus of your job search needs to be on interpersonal contacts your computer can play an important support role. The internet makes uncovering job opportunities easier than ever. As you launch your job-finding campaign, start with vertical job search engines as a destination for your customised CVs. If they are not producing needed results you should try niche job boards. A job board is a website where you can look for a job. Employers pay job boards to post their open positions. Job seekers typically view job listings for free. There are several job search sites in Ireland, including www.irishjobs.ie. You can go to www.topjobsites.com to get the latest site rankings, which are published monthly. Most of the rankings are for American-based job sites, however.

Your Approach to the Job Interview

There are a few things to keep in mind as you get ready for the interview. Dress appropriately and be properly groomed. Get yourself psyched-up before you walk into the interview room. You want to make the best possible impression. Arrive in time and be sure to bring an extra copy of your CV. And don't assume the interviewer has read the documentation you submitted prior to the interview.

During the interview focus on what you can do for this potential employer. Ask the kind of questions that show you understand the needs of the organisation. There are a few things you can do to close the sale during the interview. Be prepared to answer the direct or implied question, 'What can you do for our company immediately?' Emphasise in the interview how you'll fit into the company culture.

After the interview send a brief follow-up thank-you note reaffirming your interest in the position. If you don't hear from the organisation within a reasonable time it's appropriate to make a follow-up telephone call. But don't be too pushy. And be prepared for rejection. My friend and colleague, Dr. Paul Powers, had this to say in a *New York Times* interview: 'Remember that the essential nature of an active job hunt, while you're unemployed, is rejection. If you are not getting rejected enough, you're not working hard enough.' Powers is author of *Winning Job Interviews*. He believes each interview can be a learning experience and he recommends that you conduct your own 'post-interview review'.

Consider the Self-employment Option

As you look to regain your economic security the other major option to consider is some form of self-employment. This can range from purchasing a franchise to establishing your own business to running a home-based consulting business. I'll briefly consider each of these options.

In the current economic climate, with job loss figures mounting, many people are likely to consider franchising as the easiest way to self-employment. Franchises generally have a better survival rate than businesses set up independently. The better performance by the franchises is primarily because of the support they provide the individual franchisee.

In considering a particular franchise you need to do plenty of research. When dealing with a master franchiser be sure to get independent legal and financial advice on everything that is presented to you. One of the best ways to get first-hand experience on how a franchise operation is run is to get a job in one you are interested in. If that's not possible, talk to existing franchisees. You'll generally find that the franchise community is helpful and happy to share information about what's working and what's not, and the level of support they get.

Franchising isn't for everyone. For one thing, the entry fees are prohibitive for many individuals. It's generally agreed that getting a new franchise established demands long hours and a lot of hard work. One of the advantages is that it allows you to be your own boss while also having the safety net that most franchises provide.

As you consider future possibilities another option to consider is establishing your own business, such as opening a restaurant. This can be very difficult in the current economic environment as banks are reluctant to provide the start-up funding. Again, you have to do your research before getting involved in this kind of venture. Many communities offer free workshops on How to Start Your Own Business. This kind of learning opportunity is highly desirable for anybody considering going into business for the first time. In my view, one of the most important requisites for establishing your own business is having an entrepreneurial/sales personality. It helps if you are a person with a lot of energy and drive.

As mentioned previously, there's an increasing list of online resources available to the person starting a new business. The County and City Enterprise Boards (CEBs) provide support for small businesses with 10 employees or less, at the local level. Information is available on their website, www.enterpriseboards.ie. The Department of Enterprise, Trade and Employment is devoted to growing Ireland's competitiveness and availability of quality employment. The website address is www.entemp.ie. A not-for-profit organisation called First Step provides micro-financing. For information, visit www.first-step.ie.

The Home-based Business Option

A more feasible option to consider as you work towards establishing your economic security is establishing some kind of home-based business. This could be anything from a management consultancy to a home repair business. The advantage is that the start-up costs can be relatively small. However, before embarking on this kind of venture it is critically important to do the research. Do you have a business plan? Is there a market for your product or service? Will you be able to sell that product or service? Do you have the resources to sustain you until your business turns a profit?

There are clearly some challenges in getting a home-based business established. Due to your business's inherent small size you may not have enough customers or clients to manage the financial roller coaster that can happen if you run into a financial shortfall. In a small business it does not take much to cause a financial crisis. Here are a few things to keep in mind:

- Manage your cash flow

- Keep in touch with your customers/clients

- Push your clients to pay their bills – if there is a problem collecting don't let it linger

- Be fanatical about controlling your expenses.

If you are establishing a new venture try not to go it alone. Having one or two people who will support you is essential. Sometimes it's possible to get a small group of business friends to serve as an informal advisory board.

Keep an Open Mind on Future Options

What I've suggested in this chapter is that there are several options if you are out of work and looking for a means to provide economic security for yourself and your family. For most people the favoured option will involve a job search for a nine to five job. Because there's so much competition for the few jobs available during this recession the job search needs to be very well executed. The commonsense strategies provided here are intended to give you a competitive edge in a very difficult job market.

For the more entrepreneurially minded there's the option of some form of self-employment. And, as I've pointed out, there are several possibilities for the individual who goes down this road. The most important thing as you work towards securing your future economic security is not to act out of desperation. You may have to avail of some less-than-desirable in-between opportunities to support yourself and your family until you find what you really want.

Go Forward with a Positive Attitude

As discussed in the last chapter, one of the most damaging consequences of losing a job is the impact on self-esteem. It would be easy to succumb to negative self-talk. In Chapter 3 I recommended the use of *positive affirmations* to counteract negativity in the environment. The person out in the job market could also benefit from the use of positive self-talk. It might be as simple as reminding yourself that you bring to the job market valuable skills and experience. The important thing is that you have a positive and realistic mindset. Your support network can help in this regard.

There are a number of websites that will help you as you move forward. One of these – www.losingyourjob.ie – is offered by the Citizen Information Board. It offers information for those who are currently unemployed or becoming unemployed in Ireland.

I'll end this discussion of dealing with unemployment on an upbeat note. We know this Great Recession will end. It may be two or three years but it will end. Some years ago when I was trying to cope with some challenges in my own business a friend sent me a wall plaque with the words *Hang in There!* That is the advice I pass along to everyone coping with a bleak economic situation. Just hang in there!

In the next chapter we'll move on to consider how the recession can provide the motivation for a rebalancing of life priorities.

Tips for Survival:

❖ As you negotiate your way through the grieving process after job loss, you work towards getting your head in a good place for the job search.

❖ Do your research no matter which option you are considering. Search engines such as Google are invaluable sources of information.

❖ Develop a support network. Use your friends as a sounding board.

❖ Identify and use all the resources available in your community. Your local library can be a valuable resource. Some communities offer counselling services for the unemployed.

❖ Get out of the house and stay fully engaged with society. And do at least one thing each day that will contribute towards helping you accomplish your career goal.

8

An Opportunity to Rebalance Your Life

THROUGH MY WORK AS A management psychologist on both sides of the Atlantic since the early 1980s, I've noticed a significant evolution in attitudes towards work. Increasingly work has come to dominate the lives of many individuals. *I believe one of the more positive outcomes of this Great Recession may be the fact that it will force many to rethink their values in relation to work and the other dimensions of their lives.* Maybe, as we go forward, individuals will make more time for themselves, their families and their communities. In this chapter I offer some ideas on what a reframing of life priorities might look like.

With the Industrial Revolution work came to be viewed as a necessary evil that was endured to put food on the table and to pay for shelter. This view prevailed until relatively recently. However, that view of work has changed over the last few decades. And the relationship with the workplace has changed during this time. Our age was the first in which it was assumed you'd probably work anyway, even if you didn't need the money. You worked for yourself although you were employed by a company. The idea of loyalty to the company became old-fashioned.

You followed a strategy of job-hopping if it suited your interests. It was a seller's market and companies were falling over themselves to retain staff and keep them motivated.

In response to this phenomenon management training firms started offering training seminars for managers and supervisors on *employee retention*. Employees, emulating their professional sports heroes, began to think of themselves as free agents. If they didn't feel fulfilled or self-actualised or properly compensated, they moved on. Work came to totally dominate the lives of many. In more than a few cases, the obsession with success in the workplace led people to have lots of money but no outside life. Your value as a human person was directly related to the size of your salary and your material possessions. In the boom times some became mesmerised by work. Unfortunately, careerism and materialism led many to ignore other important dimensions of life.

One of the lessons of this Great Recession is the revelation that some of the people with the biggest incomes were often greedy individuals concerned only about themselves. Lots of money didn't necessarily make them good citizens. The bank executives with their multimillion tax-supported bonus payments are a good example. But of course it was not just the bankers that got caught up in the money-making frenzy. I believe that one of the valuable outcomes of this economic crisis is the opportunity it presents to put work/career back in perspective – to make room for what I refer to as the other *life spaces*.

The Great Recession Calls for New Attitudes Towards Work/Career

Now, with this recession, attitudes towards work are quickly changing. Employees are concerned with proving their value to their employer. They want job security. A less idealistic view of work is likely to return. For many people, work will again be welcomed for its most basic function: food and shelter and survival.

Ironically, this change in attitude may come as a relief. The dominant idea of our time that you can make it, that you can do anything, led to false expectations. Of course the changing dynamics of the workplace will not be easy for some who were spoiled during the boom years. Having invested so much of their personalities in their jobs, they may feel bereft if unemployed or if working short time.

This Great Recession is a call to humility, to the recognition that there are stubborn problems in human life that will not go away, that life is not all 'peaches and cream'. In the recent past people had become somewhat divorced from reality. This was particularly true for young white-collar workers. Happiness was no longer something they had a right to search for, but something they were entitled to. They had these norms of the perfect self-actualised life, but we will always fall short of that. The expectations became unrealistic. They began to live beyond their means. This phenomenon is referred to by Aileen Doyle and Phyllis Brennan in their Chapter 1 sidebar.

Towards a More Realistic View of Work

Back in the 1950s, American psychologist Abraham Maslow introduced the idea of a Hierarchy of Needs. At the bottom of Maslow's hierarchy was the basic need for food and shelter. There are other higher level needs but at the top of the hierarchy was the need to be fully self-actualised. Not too many get to this level. However, as I've indicated, during the years leading up to this recession many were looking to have their higher level of needs satisfied in the workplace. Now, with the Great Recession, more than a few have come tumbling back down to the bottom of Maslow's hierarchy. I'm not insinuating that there's anything wrong in striving to become self-actualised. It's just that these bleak economic times demand more realistic and pragmatic expectations.

In asserting that we may have in recent years developed some unrealistic expectations about work I'm not suggesting that we go back to a time when workers were *owned* by the company. In New England, my home base for several decades, there are old mills and factories where, in the nineteenth century, young women worked for 60 hours a week for a subsistence allowance. In the words of the old Paul Robson song, 'they owed their souls to the company store'. We certainly don't want to go back there. What's needed now is a new relationship between employee and employer that's based on mutual self-interest.

ℬ ℬ ℬ

Jean Roberts:

Put a Priority on the
Quality of Your Lifestyle

'*For more than a decade in the 1980s and throughout the 1990s my husband and I were involved as owners in growing a technology company based in South Dublin. We were operating in an extremely challenging economic environment. In reflecting back on that experience the advice I would give to business owners who are dealing with the challenges of the current recession is that, despite the pressures, they take time out for themselves. Even a short vacation can do wonders for your perspective!*

After winding up our business I established a home-based consultancy offering both in-house and public training seminars. My husband pursued research in the field of anthropology. The move from the business rat-race in the city to the country made for a much healthier lifestyle. We now enjoy the comfort of a wood-burning stove that's fuelled with firewood from our own property. We have more time for family and friends. And we have time to cultivate fruit and vegetables in our garden.

My new liberated lifestyle gives me the opportunity to work with my good friend Rosemarie Mason from the UK in promoting HANDLE throughout Ireland. HANDLE (Holistic Approach to Neurodevelopment and Learning Efficiency – www.handle.org) is a wonderful organisation dedicated to helping people with recognised special needs (e.g. Autism Spectrum Disorders, etc.). It is also helpful for those of us who are not as free from stress as we would like to be. In the current climate it can be beneficial to many of us.

My advice is to use this recession as incentive to look at ways that you can improve the quality of your lifestyle and to explore ways to be of service to others.'

(Jean Roberts is owner of Ildana Training. She is also administrator for HANDLE® Ireland.)

ℭ ℭ ℭ

Towards a More Balanced Lifestyle – The LifeSpace Grid

As indicated above, in the pursuit of their career many neglected other important dimensions of life. In my 1995 book, *Creating the Resilient Organization*, I describe a LifeSpace Grid developed in collaboration with a colleague. The four-space grid was designed to illustrate the four life-spaces in a well balanced life - self, family, community and career. Figure 1 below shows a life that is dominated by career at the expense of self, family and community. While career is clearly the dominant space in the lives of many people, I believe the Great Recession offers the opportunity to re-evaluate priorities with a view to living a more balanced life with more time for family and community.

First, you need to make sure your life has *personal space*. There's growing evidence that Americans are working longer hours than they were just one decade ago. And they take by far the shortest vacations in the industrialised world. Many limit themselves to taking off a couple of long weekends. Clearly, for most people a long weekend is not enough to fully unwind and restore mind and spirit. While workers in Ireland and the UK put a higher priority on holiday time, there seems to be a trend towards working longer hours. A survey of 1,000 adults by recruitment firm Office Angels in 2009 showed that one in five Irish workers admitted that work had taken precedence over their personal lives in the past year.

Figure 1: The LifeSpace Grid

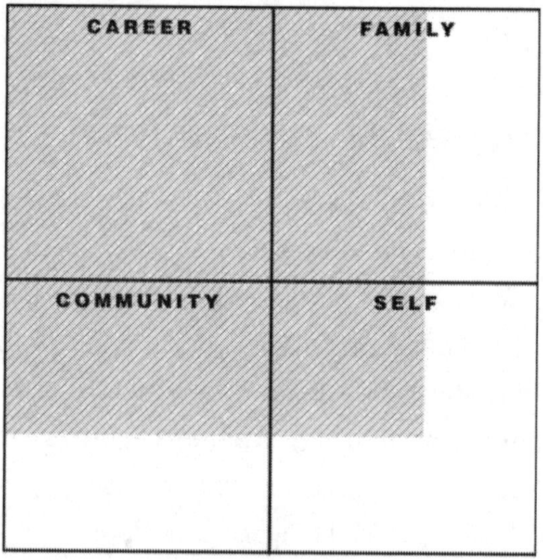

A life with *personal space* implies taking time away from work to renew the spirit. It suggests making time for regular daily exercise. And it suggests making time to take care of your own emotional and spiritual needs. This could include yoga, meditation or time with a good book. Paying attention to your 'inner spirit' can be most helpful in today's hectic world. And being conscious of *living in the present moment* can also be rewarding. Deborah Dooley, in her Chapter 2 sidebar, has an interesting but slightly unconventional recipe for nurturing oneself and coping with the stress of the recession.

A balanced life also calls for *family space*. With both parents working long hours, traditional family life has almost disappeared over the past couple of decades. A balanced life that includes family space suggests quality time with children. It suggests that individuals and organisations consider introducing family-friendly working schedules. The idea of the whole family coming together for an evening meal is certainly worthy of consideration as families strive to cope with the Great Recession. At a minimum there should be quality family time during weekends.

A well-balanced life also calls for *community space*. In recent years membership in social, civic and religious organisations has declined dramatically because of work commitments. In most communities there are many opportunities to volunteer services. And the idea of reaching out to help your neighbour is good for your own psychological welfare.

ഇ ഇ ഇ

Michael Deevy:

Get Involved in Your Community

'Laois Friends of Special Needs is an advocacy group which was formed in the year 2000. Our main mission was to lobby for both children and adult respite services in County Laois. As we were the only organisation at the time advocating for these* services, it took a lot of meetings and lobbying, over a three year period, in order to have both the children and adult services provided in the county. Over the last ten years we've been engaged in many innovative projects to respond to the respite needs of families.

One such project was the establishment of monthly social evenings for adults. With the help of HSE and Lotto funding we were able to set up a pilot project, providing free bus transport, live music and appetizing refreshments. The numbers attending the social evenings has grown to over sixty adults with special needs and friends. The social evenings have continued to be an outstanding success.

Recently we've gotten involved in a challenging new project. We plan to build a multi-functional centre which will provide support for home carers and social, recreation and therapeutic facilities for small groups of children or adults with special needs. Community and family groups will also be invited to make use of the centre for various events and occasions. The centre will be located adjacent to a forest plantation, which was especially designed at its inception, for recreational purposes. We are determined to go forward with this project despite the current recession.

I tell this story of the Laois Friends simply to suggest that so-called "ordinary citizens" are going to have to pick up more of the slack during the coming years. The impact of the recession on public spending will be with us for a long time. The Government will have less money for social and community services.

What we've learned is that if you have a deserving project the community will respond by providing support. And government agencies will respond if you can persuasively make the case for what you are trying to accomplish.

My advice to people who have skills in caring for individuals and families with special needs is that they volunteer their services to some organisation that can use them. When we start coming out of this recession these individuals will be "rewarded" with employment because of their experience and demonstrated commitment to helping people in need.

I devote my free time to supporting families who have children or adults with special needs. However, there are many other areas where you can volunteer your services. If your community has a programme for homeless people you could donate several hours of your time each week to this programme. Or you could help out with some programme in your local school. My point is this: rather than complaining about the recession we need to get out there and do something constructive in the community.'

(Michael Deevy is Chairperson of Laois Friends of Special Needs.)

Note: Inclusion Ireland is the voluntary organisation working to promote the rights of people with intellectual disabilities in Ireland and to ensure their full and equal participation in society. For information go to their website – www.inclusionireland.ie.

ജ ജ ജ

With the Great Recession millions are finding themselves involuntarily living a new life outside the workplace. Some will find it a very rewarding experience to take time for themselves, their family and their community. Hopefully, one of the positive outcomes of this terrible economic disaster will be a new awareness of the fact that there's much more to life than work. Jean Roberts, in a sidebar included in this chapter, provides personal testimony to the value of moving towards a more balanced lifestyle.

The LifeSpace Grid is not intended to suggest that we give equal time and energy to each of the four spaces. The idea is to use this grid to ask yourself if you are in fact neglecting some area that deserves more of your attention. Clearly, at certain times the individual will pay more attention to one particular life space over the others.

In this chapter I've made the case for balancing your job with other dimensions of your life. I know that in advocating more time for family and community I'm going against recent trends in our culture. To some it may sound like I'm trying 'to turn back the clock'. What I'm really saying is that a 'four-square' life is more rewarding than a life devoted purely to work and making money.

In the next chapter I'll show how the Great Recession can provide the impetus for positive lifestyle changes.

Tips for Survival:

❖ Don't allow materialism and careerism to dominate your life. Balance your commitment to earning a living with commitments to self, family and community.

❖ Adjust your expectations of work taking into account the impact of the recession on work.

❖ Explore the opportunities to contribute to your local community.

❖ Work to live, don't live to work.

9

How to Develop a More Resourceful Lifestyle

IN THE LAST CHAPTER I SUGGESTED that the recession provides the opportunity to rethink personal priorities. I underscored the need to put one's job/career into proper perspective. This chapter is about making lifestyle changes that will enable you to survive and thrive in this age of austerity. These changes involve learning to make do with more limited financial resources.

Growing up in the post-war Ireland of the 1940s I have memories of the scarcity of those years. Some food items such as tea and sugar were rationed. My family survived those difficult economic times because we were almost self-sufficient. We grew our own vegetables. My mother made butter and baked bread. And my siblings and I were frequently reminded by our parents that we were growing up under much better conditions than they had experienced as children. We never felt deprived.

Just as in Ireland, people who grew up in the UK and in the United States during the years following World War Two also experienced tough economic times. It's likely that, because of the earlier experiences, older generations today are finding it easier to make the lifestyle adjustments demanded by the Great

Recession. They already know what it's like to do without a lot of luxuries. It's likely that younger people who have not experienced tough economic times will find it more difficult to adapt to a more frugal or thrifty lifestyle. The reality is that this economic crisis is causing all of us to evaluate how we are using our resources.

ℭℭℭ

Linda Desmond:

Advice to Older Irish People: Increase Your Coping Skills

'One cost savings measure during this recessionary time would be for older people to become computer literate. We are not saying that they must become adept at Publisher or Excel or that they become the next cyber techie in the modern world. It means that with just minimal skills, the older person can save money significantly on airline tickets, hotels, misc. merchandise, newspapers, postage, phone costs and music, just to name a few cost saving ideas. At present there are a number of free or very low cost computer classes for older people through VECs, the Age Action Ireland's Getting Started Programme and an Intel-sponsored intergenerational computer training held in many schools throughout Ireland. These are just a few suggestions on computer learning opportunities for older individuals.

Another important area is to take advantage of the "free" offers available to the retirees of Ireland. Probably one of the most outstanding "freebies" offered to the older Irish person, aged 66 or over, is free travel. For all the people in the Republic who have never visited the Giant's Causeway, now's your chance and at no cost. If you have a medical condition which requires assistance, a companion can also accompany you with the proper travel pass. Your spouse can accompany you if they are not yet 66. Some cities and towns offer free exercise and swim times at city/town-owned sport centres, and don't forget to get your discounts on electricity and phone usage.

With medical cards and prescription medicine being in the forefront of political dialogue, it is not an easy call yet to determine what this will mean for the older person. One cost saving measure that the older person can do now is to always request generic drug prescriptions from your doctor. Sometimes the "brand" name drugs can be double the price of the generic substitute.

This is also a time for older people to get creative. In the "best" of economic times when the interest rates on retirement accounts are high yielding, it is easy and enjoyable to make a date with a friend for lunch. When purse strings must be tightened, why not start a Luncheon Club where older friends come together in different members homes on a monthly basis? Each Lunch Club member can bring a dish to share. Low cost, great craic!'

(Linda Desmond is CEO of CARELOCAL in Dublin.)

 හ හ හ

Still Working and Making Do with Less

With this Great Recession many families are having to make significant adjustments in their lifestyle. This reality was captured in a 29 May 2008 *New York Times* article entitled 'Still Working, but Making Do with Less'. The article described the real-life implications of this recession for millions of families. These are families who have not experienced redundancies, however they may be working short time or on furlough for several days a month. They now have to make do with less income. Because so many are living on tight budgets, even a modest step down can bring hard choices. The NYT article goes on to highlight how one California family, the Ferrells, have had to make adjustments, including cutting back on dance lessons for their twin daughters. Instead of grocery shopping at a regular supermarket, Mrs. Ferrell now loads up her minivan once a month at WinCo, a giant, no-frills discount grocery chain. In Ireland, the fastest growing sector of the grocery market is led by two discount chains. People are learning to make do with less and to get more for less.

Today, families in Ireland have to make similar adjustments to those made by the Ferrells. The same is true for the UK. In a visit to the West Country in England I heard of families on the edge of poverty having to make similar downward adjustments. The reality is that many families on both sides of the Atlantic are having to make significant lifestyle changes because of a reduction in income caused by a number of different factors.

ԑᴑ ԑᴑ ԑᴑ

A Child's Response to the Recession

The mother explained how she fixed a boxed lunch for her young girl to take to school each day. One evening the child came home and complained to her mother that the other children were 'wasting' their money on buying lunches and soft drinks. 'Don't they understand that we're living through a renaissance?' she asked.

ԑᴑ ԑᴑ ԑᴑ

The suggestions provided in this chapter on making lifestyle changes are intended to be food for thought. In doing the research for this book I became more aware that a significant minority were already living a more frugal lifestyle long before the advent of this recession. I know more than a few people who grow their own vegetables and buy their clothing in secondhand or discount stores. And they don't *waste* money trying to make an impression on friends. The ideas proposed in this chapter are primarily intended for people who may need to make lifestyle changes. As suggested by Christopher Condren in his Chapter 5 sidebar, there's a lot of wasteful spending in modern society.

The first thing to state is that it's more important than ever to live within one's means. Piling up debt makes no sense in the current uncertain economic environment. You may need to trash some of those credit cards. One helpful development is the fact that conspicuous consumption is no longer viewed as favourably as it was just a few years ago.

Individuals and families in serious debt should seek the services of one of those agencies that offer counselling in this area. In Ireland most cities and towns have a MABS (Money Advice and Budgeting Service – www.mabs.ie) office. Because of the recession many of the MABS offices have significant waiting lists of six to eight weeks. Similar services are available in the UK and the United States. Ordinarily these agencies offer their services at no charge or for a small fee. They can often help you renegotiate payment terms with bill collectors. They can also advise you on how you may be able to renegotiate mortgage payments.

Tips for Resourceful Living

Here are six tips that can help you manage your financial resources during this recession:

- *Cut your spending.* Make this a priority. Weigh up whether you really need that new flat-screen TV, and maybe going on an expensive holiday can wait one more year. Making sacrifices at this time and living realistically on a tighter budget will leave you better off in the long run.

- *Reduce your debts.* Pay a lump sum on your credit card, and reduce any loan repayments. Make sure that you are paying the lowest rate possible on any borrowing you have. Many communities have credit unions and these are worth checking out. Paddy O'Brien makes the case for joining a local credit union in his sidebar in Chapter 10. Again, as already indicated, there are professional resources available in most communities to provide advice in this area.

- *Slash your bills.* Make sure you are on the cheapest deals for your gas and electricity. Consider a wood-burning stove if you have access to free or cheap firewood. If you have a mobile phone or broadband see if there are cheaper options available. Chances are, if you have been on the same deal for more than two years then you can cut your bill. If you have a mobile phone consider if you still need to be paying for that land line.

- *Put money away for a rainy day and make sure you have a cushion of cash savings.* I mentioned in Chapter 6 the wisdom of having an Emergency Fund that would cover three to six months of basic expenses.

- *Re-negotiate your mortgage payments.* Normally, when a recession strikes, interest rates are cut. This can be good news for homeowners as it means the price of tracker mortgages will fall. Individuals who lose their jobs should contact their bank or mortgage company to see if they can negotiate better terms for payments. You will find useful information on the website of the Financial Regulator – www.itsyourmoney.ie.

- *Don't change jobs.* Companies make cutbacks when their profits get hit and staff are usually the first to be axed from the balance sheet. New employees can often be the first in the firing line.

More Ideas on Managing Your Personal or Family Budget

When it comes to managing your personal or family budget there are many ideas that can be considered. The list I offer here is only intended to give an indication of the kinds of things you might do to help with your budget situation. If you are one of those 'shop till I drop' individuals you may find it difficult to embrace some of these suggestions. Old habits are difficult to change! Anyway, here's a list of additional suggestions:

- *Don't buy things simply because they are a good deal.* And if you have a garage full of stuff you never use you might consider putting some of it on eBay or bringing it to a car boot sale.

- *Don't ignore bills.* If you have a large utility bill call the company and negotiate a payment plan you can afford. If you are in dire straits just make a very small payment to each of your creditors. In some instances this strategy can keep the wolves from the door.

- *Spend less than you earn.* The basic idea is to take a conservative approach to spending.

- *Do whatever you can to increase your earning ability.* This might require getting some additional training.

- *Explore all possibilities for increasing income.* This might involve providing some home-based services to neighbours. Think 'outside of the box' – the possibilities are endless.

- *Reduce your utility bills.* If you turn down your thermostat it can make a big difference on your monthly bill. Also insulating your house is an idea to consider. Up to 30 per cent of the heat in your house can be lost through the roof. One of the most basic things to do is turning off lights when they are not needed.

- *Shop around for the best food prices.* There is no shame in going to a discount store. Those expensive brands that are heavily advertised on television and in the newspapers are usually no better than the generic store brands. You pay for all that advertising.

- *Buy generic prescriptions.* They are cheaper and are generally just as good as those brands you see advertised on television.

These are just a sample of things to do. There are many others that a family can do to help get through this recession. I have several friends who have taken up the example of Michelle Obama and now have productive gardens. One neighbour contacted me about offering ironing services. Another does minor house repairs for people in the community. And another cleans house windows for her neighbours. The recession offers opportunities for entrepreneurial endeavours at the personal and family level.

ဢ ဢ ဢ

Five Healthy Tips to Beat the Credit Crunch

1. ***Buy in season.*** *It's always cheaper to buy fruit and vegetables in season. Keep an eye out for bargains in your local supermarket. Don't be tempted to throw out fresh vegetables – use them up to make a pot of delicious and nutritious soup.*

2. ***Grow your own veg.*** *Even if you don't have a large garden, you can quickly cut your food bills by growing your own fruit and veg. A few pots on the patio or a window box will do the job.*

3. ***Do your own housework.*** *You can save lots of money on cleaners by doing household jobs yourself. As well as reducing costs, tasks like cleaning windows, washing the car and vacuuming will give you a great physical work out.*

4. ***Make your own healthy lunch and get moving.*** *Why not enjoy a healthy homemade packed lunch and a brisk walk instead of eating a shop-bought sandwich at your desk? It's healthier and it's cheaper.*

5. ***Cycle or walk to work.*** *Leaving your car behind and cycling or walking to work is a relaxing and energetic alternative. Or if you use public transport, get off one or two stops before and walk the remaining distance. You'll save a little cash and get some exercise in too.*

(Reprinted with permission from Easy Health, *Autumn 2008, www.easyhealthandliving.com)*

ဢ ဢ ဢ

In summary, there are many ways of cutting living and entertainment costs without significantly impacting on the quality of your lifestyle. Some people will do more home entertaining rather than going to expensive restaurants. Linda Desmond has several cost-saving ideas for older Irish citizens in her sidebar in this chapter. Families may choose holidays that involve less travel. The key survival strategy involves living within one's means.

In the next chapter I'll offer a few guidelines for people facing the nightmare scenario, namely, bankruptcy or the possibility of losing their home.

Tips for Survival:

❖ Develop a personal/family budget – and live within this budget.

❖ If you have serious debt, consider using the services of a nonprofit agency that offers advisory services.

❖ Avoid piling up credit card debt – live within your means.

❖ Stop wasteful spending and avoid conspicuous consumption.

❖ Enjoy the challenge!

10

Dealing with the
Worst Case Scenario

WHAT DO YOU DO WHEN you're facing bankruptcy or fore-closure becomes a possibility? How do you dig yourself out of a deep financial hole? While this is not a book on financial management, I'll briefly address these questions in this chapter.

The laws governing bankruptcy vary from country to country. In some cases declaring bankruptcy may be the best option. It's important to work with a credit counselling agency as you attempt to cope with a serious financial situation. As I indicated in the last chapter, the services of such an agency are generally available at no cost or for very little. This kind of agency serves as an *objective party* to help you sort through your problems. They will provide you with personalised budgeting advice and design a customised plan to get you out of debt.

You can also be proactive yourself in coming up with solutions to your credit problems. There are some good books available providing advice on financial management. In the United States, Susie Orman has developed a reputation as a guru in this field. However, some critics would say that Orman and the other financial pundits on cable television totally failed to see the financial crash coming. It's a fair criticism. *I urge caution in dealing with anyone who is selling financial products at this time.* Avoid services with a financial interest in what you are doing. If possible, seek advice from individuals who are in a position to offer you purely *objective* guidance.

Beware of the Greedy Money Lenders

Before going on to discuss strategies for coping with bankruptcy and foreclosure, it's worth reminding ourselves of why so many are now in such dire financial straits. Put simply, the problems that many individuals and families are dealing with today are the result of the greed of money lenders. This idea was highlighted by Jonathan Freedland in his commentary in the 22 July 2009 edition of *The Guardian*. Freedland wrote about how a rabbi, an iman and a priest visited the headquarters of the Royal Bank of Scotland in the City of London to present three books to the Chairman of the Company: the Torah, the Qur'an and the New Testament. This symbolic visit was intended as a warning to the titans of finance that a campaign is coming, in both Britain and the United States, aimed at changing the way banks do business by reviving a law as old as money itself.

The law in question is the prohibition on usury. Laws against usury date back thousands of years and are enshrined in the three sacred books presented by the faith delegation. These laws limited the amount a lender could charge and clearly indicated that to charge too much interest is immoral. Ironically, the laws against usury were relaxed in the not too distant past. We now see the results with greed running out of control with little government regulation. One of the most recent expressions of this greed in the United States involves loan modification scams.

Normally, homeowners seek loan modifications in hopes of forestalling foreclosure. However, scam artists have seized the opportunity to use phony loan modification schemes to prey on vulnerable borrowers. The real unfortunate aspect of the foreclosure rescue scams is that it makes an already stressful and tough situation more stressful and more difficult.

Unscrupulous individuals are targeting at-risk homeowners by combing foreclosure notices in newspapers, the internet and public files to identify potential victims, according to the Federal Trade Commission in the US.

Some of the scam artists are the people who sold the original mortgages. According to a 20 July 2009 *New York Times* article, many of the companies in Southern California that made millions selling risky mortgages during the real estate boom have found a new way to make millions. They have reconstituted themselves into a new industry focused on selling loan modifications. Despite making promises of relief to homeowners desperate to keep their homes, the *New York Times* investigation found they often fail to deliver. After getting upfront fees of one to three thousand dollars they move on leaving the homeowner more desperate than before. The same people who sold the original mortgages have found a new way to cash in.

Evan Greer, in his commentary included in Chapter 6, makes no secret about his feelings towards those greedy individuals who exploit the vulnerable. As I read his piece I wondered how many would share his sentiments. Maybe more than we expect.

I mention the greed of money lenders and scam artists because people in serious financial trouble need to know what they are up against. And I'm not sure the campaign by the faith leaders who visited the headquarters of the Bank of Scotland will have much impact. Don't expect much sympathy when you go to your mortgage lender. And despite all the talk, few politicians have the spine to take on the bankers and other money lenders.

Healthcare Costs Are a Major Problem

There are a number of reasons why a person can end up bankrupt. In the United States one of the major causes of bankruptcy is healthcare costs. Fortunately, in Ireland and the UK people are less likely to be bankrupted by healthcare costs.

A study by Harvard University researchers, published in the August 2009 edition of the *American Journal of Medicine*, found that medical bills, plus related problems such as lost wages for the ill and their caregivers, contributed to 62 per cent of all bankruptcies filed in the United States in 2007. According to the same study medical insurance isn't much help, either. About 78 per cent of bankruptcy filers burdened by healthcare expenses were insured.

Most people who filed medical-related bankruptcies 'were solidly middle class before financial disaster hit', the study says. Two-thirds were homeowners and most had gone to college.

Obviously, this Harvard University study is based on data collected before the current recession. It's fair to assume that the situation has gotten much worse since that time with more families having to declare bankruptcy. And clearly there are other factors, including joblessness, that are causing a financial crisis for many individuals and families on both sides of the Atlantic.

ജ   ജ   ജ

Paddy O'Brien:

Why You Should Consider Joining Your Local Credit Union

To date in Ireland over 2.9 million members have recognised the benefits and values of credit unions and have savings approaching €11.9 billion. There are over 9,200 active volunteers involved in the movement and over 3,300 people employed.

It has been shown throughout history that by working together people can achieve far more through cooperation than by individual effort.

I would strongly encourage all families in today's financial turmoil to consider joining your local credit union and to encourage young people to save and build up a good credit rating. This will enable you to borrow money at a reasonable rate ... and this is very important because most other financial institutions are not lending to individuals or to businesses.

There are more than 500 credit unions all over Ireland where you can become an active member and borrow money and steer clear of money-lenders charging exorbitant interest rates. You will not be charged for any hidden services at your credit union and will not be penalised if you pay off your loan early.

The benefits of being a member of a credit union include a simple loan application process and quick decisions on great value low interest loans. Again, no hidden fees or transaction charges. You share in any surplus your credit union makes by way of a yearly dividend payment.

The Irish credit union movement was founded back in the 1950s as a result of people experiencing the effects of high unemployment, sickness, poor housing, hunger and, of course, for many it was emigration. In addition, state benefits were low leaving many families in abject poverty.

The founders of the credit union movement recognised the root of the problem as lying in the scarce availability and poor management of money. They resolved to come up with a system that would allow people to gain more control over their finances.

It is worth noting that many individuals and families today are facing challenges similar to those faced by our parents and grandparents back in the 1950s. That's why I am so strongly recommending that individuals and families consider availing of the services provided by their local credit union.

A credit union is an organisation of people for people. Its ethos is to serve its members – not to profit from their needs. Credit unions are non-sectarian and non-political, and continue that Irish tradition of free life savings and loan protection insurance. All members are treated equally and confidentially. And credit unions put people before profits.

I understand that one of the themes of this book is that "the Great Recession" presents us not merely with challenges but also with opportunities. In my view, a more sensible approach to money management would be one valuable lesson.'

(Paddy O'Brien is a Credit Union Volunteer in Kilnamanagh, Dublin 24.)

ℰ ℰ ℰ

Coping with the Threat of Foreclosure

Unfortunately, with this Great Recession foreclosure looms for many families. The loss of a job can become catastrophic as couples become overwhelmed with mortgage payments. We now know that many families were over-extended before this recession and were totally dependent on the income generated by both spouses. The loss of a job by one spouse can spell disaster.

As soon as you begin to sense that your financial situation has taken a turn for the worse, you and the rest of your household need to work together to keep the problem from getting worse. To stabilise your financial situation you may have to prioritise your bills. The first order of business is to get a handle on your finances. This involves slashing unnecessary expenses. Consider making the lifestyle changes suggested in Chapter 9. And mobilise the whole family in trying to generate income. If you have children living at home explain to them why you have had to introduce an austerity budget. And by all means invite them to be part of the solution.

If you are committed to saving your home set aside the extra cash for reinstating the mortgage or working out a payment plan with the bank. If saving your house is a lost cause you should try to put away some cash to take with you when you move.

There are a number of online services that provide support for individuals who are experiencing serious financial challenges. MABS was identified as a resource in Chapter 4 and the website of the Financial Regulator – www.itsyourmoney.ie – provides information on financial products in plain English.

Develop a Plan and Seek Professional Advice

Given what I've said about the money lenders, it's even more important that you have a plan if you're facing possible foreclosure. You have to decide which option is most likely to get you back on your feet. Do you sell the house and get out from under the burden or do you live in the home for as long as possible and only move when the sheriff comes with the eviction papers? Each situation is different and needs a customised strategy.

Again, it's useful to repeat the advice given by Phyllis Brennan and Aileen Doyle in their Chapter 1 sidebar. When you're facing a major financial crisis it's essential to seek professional advice to help you explore the various options. An adviser may recommend that you file for bankruptcy, or they may recommend refinancing with another lender. It's helpful to remember that most banks don't want a lot of foreclosed houses on their books. Often these abandoned houses become vandalised and lose their value. You may be able to arrange some kind of 'deal' with the lender.

Manage Your Stress Level

The advice given in Chapter 2 on dealing with recession-related stress is particularly relevant for anyone who finds themselves in a deep financial hole. Even if you're faced with the possibility of giving up your home you need to maintain good physical and psychological health. Again, it's helpful to remember that you didn't cause the financial meltdown that has put so many in a disastrous financial situation.

Telling someone who is facing the possibility of losing their home to keep a positive attitude sounds hollow. Nevertheless, this is the time to look inside and be aware of your own coping resources. It's also the time to turn to family and friends who may be in a position to provide both financial and psychological support. This kind of challenge calls for a resilient response. Sometimes local organisations, including churches, are in a position to provide tangible support. When the going gets tough it's okay to reach out to others for a helping hand. If you are feeling overwhelmed you might consider calling the *Samaritans* or some other organisation providing emergency support.

ᔓ ᔓ ᔓ

Help in Time of Emergency: The Samaritans

Samaritans provide confidential non-judgemental emotional support, 24 hours a day for people who are experiencing distress or despair, including those that could lead to suicide. (Phone: Republic of Ireland: 1850 609090; UK: 08457 909090)

ᔓ ᔓ ᔓ

In the next chapter I'll summarise the major lessons of this book in a list of Do's and Don'ts.

Tips for Survival:

❖ If you are facing bankruptcy seek the advice of a credit counselling agency.

❖ If foreclosure looms engage the services of a professional to explore the various options available.

❖ Proactively manage your stress level as you deal with the challenge of coping with bankruptcy and/or foreclosure.

❖ If you are feeling overwhelmed by the situation consider calling the *Samaritans* or some other organisation providing emergency support services.

11

The Great Recession Survival Checklist

THE THEME OF THIS BOOK IS THAT we need proactive strategies to deal with the psychological and economic challenges posed by the Great Recession. The ideas put forward are designed to promote individual and family resilience. I believe that, despite the difficult challenges, it's important to maintain a positive 'can do' attitude.

In this chapter I bring together a checklist of the key do's and don'ts for surviving this era of economic turmoil. Identify those items on the list that are most relevant to your situation.

Here's the list of Do's:

- *Manage the fear that comes from dealing with an uncertain future.* Don't allow yourself to be crippled by fear or negativity.

- *Surround yourself with positive people.* And when you are getting totally depressed by all the bad economic news on television turn to another channel or find something more interesting to do with your time.

- *Be proactive in dealing with your financial situation.* If the problem is dealt with as soon as possible the consequences are far more likely to be manageable. And if you get into serious trouble seek the services of professional financial advisers. There are nonprofit organisations that offer these services.

- *Keep yourself physically fit and healthy.* This includes maintaining a proper diet and regular daily exercise. This will serve as an antidote to recession-related stress.

- *Take responsibility for your personal and/or family budget.* This includes living within your means. If you can, put some money aside for the 'rainy day'.

- *Maintain a positive 'can do' attitude.* Say no to cynicism and pessimism.

- *Make necessary lifestyle changes.* You can still have a quality lifestyle while spending less.

- *Develop/maintain a support network.* This applies whether you have a job or are looking for a job.

- *Think outside the box.* This is especially applicable for individuals who find themselves joining the ranks of the unemployed. The Great Recession has the potential to open up possibilities you never thought about before.

- *Be patient and don't panic.* No point in beating up on yourself because the global financial system has crashed.

- *Continue to have space for fun and recreation in your life.* Keep yourself psychologically healthy so that you are better able to beat the recession.

- *Be friendly and helpful to others.* Provide support for your neighbour who may be in a more challenging situation than you are. If you've lost your nine to five job, volunteer your services. Stay fully engaged with life!

- *Do things that are good for your soul.* Michael Roberts, in his sidebar below, makes the case that Irish people during these challenging times need to rediscover their spiritual values and their cultural heritage.

ဢ ဢ ဢ

Michael Roberts:

We Need to Rediscover Spiritual Values

'As we negotiate our way through this period of economic turmoil it is a good time to rediscover some of our spiritual values and heritage. Let me explain.

Each age and strategy has its own spirit. In the late 1800s the spirit of individualism and freedom was dominant. This was closely connected to the colonial spirit, a program of adventure and entrepreneurial expansion. The western world felt it had a right to conquer the eastern and southern worlds and to take profit and power at their expense. Military machines were the technology of conquest.

One hundred years later and the same spirit emerged again with modern technology as the tools of conquest. International communications using modern transport and TV, radio, telecommunications and computers enabled the western world to dominate world commerce. Young people, high on the spirit of individualism, ego and freedom, played games with the welfare of the world watched over by senior citizens who should have known better and, perhaps, did.

In each case greed and selfishness predominated while the spirit of respect and community were muted. The result was catastrophic for the vast majority of people, ordinary people trying to make a worthwhile life for themselves and for their children. A small few became very wealthy.

The spirit of equality and fair play was lost, smothered in a blanket of disrespect and neglect.

Today, many people are feeling dispirited. With a world-wide loss of charitable intent, economic downturn, the scandal of war in the east and the scandals within the churches, many people have lost the hope and faith to generate and sustain a decent way of life.

Just a short few years ago many people were optimistic and joyful. The world seemed to live up to the spirit of great promise made to all who educated themselves, worked hard and treated their neighbour with respect and dignity, who did the "right things", could live happily and be prosperous. But, this has now changed. Selfishness and greed have become the norm as we all over-reached ourselves in an attempt to be self-fulfilled. Our spirit failed. Where did it all go wrong?

What do we mean when we talk about the spirit of our times? Is this some mood that is generated by the excitement of our activities or is it something else, something of a deeper part of our nature? In the "good ol' days" we talked about the spirit of good and evil, of God and the Devil, but today that language seems inappropriate and out-dated.

I am suggesting we all might use this challenging time to re-discover transcendent spiritual values. We need a new "Spirit of our Time". The process of rediscovery is more likely to emerge out of grassroots discussions between family and friends.'

(Dr. Michael Roberts is an anthropologist living in Sligo.)

ဆာ ဆာ ဆာ

There are a few things you don't want to do as you mobilise your resources to survive this recession. Here's the list of Don'ts:

- *Don't blame yourself.* Okay, the bottom fell out of the economy but it's not your fault.

- *Don't waste your resources.* Living a more frugal lifestyle does not mean the end of the world! Think of it as an opportunity to refocus on those things that are really important in life

- *Don't take on unnecessary debt.* Despite what the economists say, these times call for saving, not spending.

- *Don't think or talk like a victim.* A negative mindset will greatly handicap your efforts to cope with this recession. And don't believe the negative messages you are picking up from radio and television.

- *Don't give up 'working' even if you have joined the ranks of the unemployed.* You still need to be fully engaged with life.

- *Don't have unrealistic expectations, especially if you are out searching for a job.* It is likely that we are all going to have to cope with a bleak economic environment for several years.

- *Don't expect easy solutions* – it will be tough. Hang in there!

There are other items that you can add to these checklists. The key point I want to communicate is that you need to keep yourself psychologically in a good place if you are to successfully cope with the challenges posed by the Great Recession. To use a sports metaphor, you need to keep yourself fighting fit. And you also need to take a commonsense approach to managing your personal and family finances. Live within your budget and make the lifestyle changes that are necessary.

Finally, I'd like to reaffirm the idea that this recession has the potential to bring out the best in all of us. We are already learning to make do with less. We're beginning to ask some basic questions about what's really important in life. And the recession is inspiring a new resilient spirit in many individuals and families. One mother told me she would not allow this economic crisis to damage the ambitions of her children. That's the kind of attitude that's needed to survive the Great Recession.

Tips for Survival:

- ❖ As you go forward don't allow yourself to be crippled by fear or negativity.

- ❖ Manage your response to the Great Recession – don't allow yourself to think or act like a victim.

- ❖ Keep yourself in good shape – physically and psychologically.

- ❖ Be empathetic to others.

12

Moving Forward:
How to Keep Hope Alive!

THE NOTED UNITED STATES civil rights leader Jesse Jackson coined the expression, *Keep Hope Alive!* Having worked in the Deep South in the civil rights movement in the 1960s, I know the message that Jackson was delivering to his people. He was offering the hope of a better life to a people who had suffered severe economic deprivation for many generations. The Reverend Jackson understood the importance of letting people know that, despite present circumstances, they should be focused on the possibility of a better life in the future. Like all great leaders, he has a profound understanding of human psychology.

Winston Churchill also understood the need to hold out the hope for a better future for people going through difficult times. In 1940, when he became prime minister of the UK at one of the darkest moments in its history, he famously declared to the House of Commons that 'I have nothing to offer but blood, toil, tears, and sweat'. Though Churchill's grim phrase is remembered, it is often forgotten that he went on to offer much more. He promised 'victory in spite of all terrors' and announced that 'I take up my task in buoyancy and hope'. Clearly, his speech inspired his people to endure great hardships and to make sacrifices. A relative who was a nurse in London during the blitz often talked about the Churchill-inspired resilience of the British people during those difficult times.

US President Barack Obama also understands the need to hold out hope for a better future. In a speech to students at Georgetown University in Washington, DC, Obama explained in detail why people have to make sacrifices and why these sacrifices will ultimately result in better living conditions for the American people.

In referencing these three visionary leaders I want to highlight the fact that we need *to keep hope alive* as we go through this recession. And we need visionary leadership at every level to keep this hope alive.

ॐ   ॐ   ॐ

Mary McVeigh:

Let's Inspire Our Children with Positive Messages!

'Our children's future is literally in our arms and in our words. Tread gently as you tread on our children's dreams. Don't stunt youth's natural exuberance and energy for a brighter future for all.

We are all challenged by the constant flow of negative financial information about the economic crisis. In many cases this has affected us personally. Our children are extremely vulnerable to this bombardment of depressing facts. Children *are absorbing the full impact and assuming their futures are stained. If you ask a child what they think of the economy ... be prepared for a more informed answer than you thought.*

As adults we know the recession is not forever. There is much more to life than money —the Joy of Love — a healthy body — wonderful relationships — nature's miracles, etc.

Children are born with an overflowing reservoir of positivity; this must be cherished, not extinguished by your fears. With the current barrage of negativity are we stunting this fountain of youth? Our reactions to this recession, verbal and non-verbal, are being decoded by our children, in a very negative atmosphere, influencing their personal futures.

The realism of our dismal economic climate must be tempered with positive words and actions. The very real media driven images must be counterbalanced with positive bite-sized information that is appropriate to a child's maturation level of emotional and social development. Too much uncensored un-contextualised direct access to negative images of society and the economy will darken their vision of this beautiful world with its abundant opportunities.

Children are now having to cope with processing such information with its "no hope" scenarios. Their views will be as negative as ours if we don't embrace this period of our lives and challenge it in new directions.

All adults have a vital role to play in challenging our youth's minds along more positive lines; to do otherwise is to neglect our duty. Childhood is a time of acceptance. A casual comment can be misunderstood or misinterpreted. What we say and what they hear are two vastly different things.

As adults we have a duty to grow our children – they are more important and a greater source of happiness than any set of figures about financial growth! You can start right now with renewed optimism strengthened with the wisdom from that old adage – Many of life's greatest opportunities come into our lives disguised as problems.'

(Mary McVeigh is a parent and educator from Carbury, County Kildare.)

ɛͻ   ɛͻ   ɛͻ

A Need to Believe in Future Possibilities

One of the themes of this book is the need to believe in ourselves and in future possibilities. We need to maintain a positive outlook. We need to reject cynicism and defeatism. And we need visionary leaders who will serve as our role models.

These times call for political leaders like Winston Churchill who are capable of rallying people to make necessary sacrifices now in order to enjoy a better future. And we need political leaders who are willing to invest in the future. Consider Roosevelt's New Deal which pumped money into public works in order to keep people employed. The New Deal put America to work. People built schools, roads, ports, bridges, dams, sports stadia. Roosevelt set millions to work building marvellous things that still survive and are loved today by the American people. The Great Recession calls for this kind of courage and visionary leadership on the part of our political leaders.

Business leaders also have a role to play. They need to 'rally the troops' with the promise of more economic security in the future. There's also a need for visionary leadership at the family and community levels – leaders that are resourceful and stress future possibilities. In particular we need parents and teachers who will communicate a hopeful message to children who are barraged by all the negativity in the media on a daily basis. This message is eloquently communicated by Mary McVeigh in the sidebar above. In the United States, during World War Two, community people organised *victory gardens*. A similar community effort was undertaken in the UK. That's the kind of spirit we need to get us through this difficult period.

My vision is that we'll come out of this Great Recession with a new set of values and priorities. We'll reject the careerism and materialism that have characterised our societies for the past few decades. Hopefully, we won't put such a high value on conspicuous consumption. And some will rediscover that service to community is a noble idea.

In a graduation speech at Arizona State University, President Obama spoke about the need for 'a fundamental change of perspective and attitude, one that values substance over appearance, character over celebrity and wise investments over get rich quick schemes'. Referring to the economic crisis he had this to say: 'In recent years, in many ways, we've become enamoured with our own success, lulled into complacency by our own achievements. We started taking shortcuts. We started living on credit, instead of building up savings.'

I'm encouraged by the possibility that we as a society will learn from some of the mistakes of the past. Hopefully, the media will no longer celebrate those who are the most greedy and narcissistic in our society. It seems like a long time ago since President John Kennedy called for patriotic endeavour with these words in his inaugural speech: 'Ask not what your country can do for you but what you can do for your country.' With all the recent reports of corporate corruption I can understand why some might react cynically to this kind of call for patriotic sacrifice. But a cynical response is not the answer to our current challenges.

As we move forward we'll eventually be able to put the Great Recession in the rear view mirror. With a bit of positive psychology and some commonsense survival strategies we will come out of it stronger and more resilient individuals.

Tips for Survival:

❖ During this recession parents need to keep the vision of a more hopeful future in front of their children.

❖ Our political leaders need to inspire and motivate – not act as prophets of doom.

❖ We need visionary leadership at the community level to help address many of the social problems arising out of the Great Recession.

❖ Each of us needs to take up the challenge of beating this recession.

Afterword:
The Great Recession Revisited

O N THE MORNING OF 23 JULY 2009, I went to Dublin Airport to meet my friend Rosemary who is a hospital administrator in the Commonwealth of Virginia in the United States. Rosemary, a former client, had come to Ireland for a brief visit.

As we travelled into the city centre on the lower deck of Dublin Bus No 41 I was bringing my friend up-to-date on my book project.

'It feels great to have the first draft completed – I believe I can meet the publisher's deadline,' I said, as I pulled a copy of the manuscript from my briefcase and started to give Rosemary an outline of the key themes in each chapter.

'What motivated you to write this book?' asked Rosemary.

'I'm just tired of the daily drumbeat of negativity in the media. People need to start thinking more positively about how they can get out of this situation. Of course the greedy bankers were the root cause of our economic problems and the politicians were short-sighted not to see what was coming.'

We chatted about how the recession was affecting people in the United States and in Ireland as the bus slowly made its way

towards the city centre. Our conversation was suddenly interrupted by a woman sitting immediately behind who was obviously overhearing our conversation. She tapped me on the
shoulder and I looked around.

'I'm a single mother and you don't understand what I'm going through. And Brian Lenihan, the finance minister, doesn't
understand. He wants to take money from my children and give
it to the bankers. Why should anyone be positive about what's
happening? That positive Pollyanna stuff is not going to put
food on my table.'

For the next five minutes we listened to a non-stop rant as
this woman expressed her anger and frustration. My response
was to simply say that I understood where she was coming
from.

The woman got off the bus at Parnell Square, one stop before our destination. The whole experience was something of a
reality check.

'You know, Ed, you would hear the same sentiments expressed by millions of people in the United States. Many have
lost their jobs. People everywhere seem to be angry with the
politicians. But – I agree – it's not really helpful to get bogged
down in the negativity.'

We both concluded it had been a valuable learning experience.

Many Are Edging Towards Poverty

Two days after the encounter with the woman on Dublin Bus
Number 41 I read an article by Kathy Sheridan in the *Irish*

Times (25 July 2009) that echoed the sentiments that had been expressed. Sheridan quoted sources from within several charitable organisations in suggesting that some people might be sliding back into the kind of poverty described by the late Frank McCourt in *Angela's Ashes*. The following quotation by a social worker, included in the Sheridan article, spoke to a situation that's causing hardship for many:

> 'It's bad out there. Really bad. People may not be starving but there are plenty who have seen a really drastic change in their circumstances. Their homes are threatened, their cars have been repossessed, their furniture has been repossessed. For seven or eight years, up to a year ago, people lived in a culture of no-tomorrow, of plastic money, of lending institutions firing money around willy-nilly and now reality is beginning to bite.
>
> And I can tell you, it's causing untold stress, hardship and disharmony... Two or three years ago, these people were concerned with where they'd go on their fourth or fifth holiday, now they're concerned about the next bill coming through the door. Look at the people claiming welfare benefits – that has a snowball effect inside the home believe me.'

Let me again say that in writing this book I didn't want to downplay what's happening 'out there'. As the social worker said, things are really bad for some people. The reality is that many are suffering serious hardship as a result of this economic downturn. As repeatedly stated throughout this book – the solution lies in *how we respond* to this situation.

The Resilient Response

As I worked on this book I encountered outrage and anger directed towards anyone perceived as having a role in creating the financial meltdown. Some wondered how I could write a book like this given the amount of greed and corruption that has been revealed. But I also encountered an extraordinarily positive response from people, including the sixteen individuals who graciously agreed to share their insights on how to cope with the challenges of the recession. Indeed, one of the personal rewards of writing this book was the encouragement provided by many people who believe we need to get beyond all the negativity.

Everyone I asked to contribute an opinion piece gladly obliged. I could have gotten 100 contributors! One of my Kilnamanagh neighbours, Andrew Connors, when he heard I was working on this project, put an envelope with the following poem in my mailbox:

> I love my land,
> My native Land.
> I love it right full well.
> I love its bright and sparkling brooks.
> Both mountain vale and dell,
> But best of all I love the place
> Where first I saw the light.
> It's that lovely village Hollyford.
> My home my heart's delight.

I surmised that Andrew believed that a little patriotism would go a long way in meeting the challenges of the recession.

This is a sentiment that I heard expressed by more than a few people as I did the research for this book.

℃ ℃ ℃

The Society of St Vincent de Paul:

Working to Create a More Caring Society

The Society of St Vincent de Paul is the largest voluntary, charitable organisation in Ireland. Its membership of 9,500 volunteers throughout the country is supported by professional staff, working for social justice and the creation of a more just caring society. This network of social concern also gives practical support to those experiencing poverty and social exclusion, by providing a wide range of services to people in need. Go to the website – www.svp.ie/contact-Us.aspx - for information on local offices or to volunteer your services. Information on making a donation is also available at this site.

℃ ℃ ℃

You Can be Part of the Solution

In the early 1970s I managed a VISTA project in Louisiana. The VISTA volunteers were young Americans who set aside one year after college to work in impoverished communities. Their motto was, *If you are not part of the solution, you are part of the problem.* My hope is that this book will inspire more people to be 'part of the solution' as we cope with this Great Recession.

The media can help by focusing on the constructive things people are doing to get through these difficult times.

As mentioned in Chapter 6, there are many opportunities to volunteer your time. Charitable organisations serving people in need have an even greater need for volunteers and resources because of the impact of the recession. A sidebar included in Chapter 10 provides information on the Samaritans. The St. Vincent de Paul Society is having to respond to the needs of many more people than at any previous time. In Dublin the Simon Community is one of several organisations serving the homeless. Similar charitable organisations operate in most communities in the UK and in the United States. All these voluntary organisations are helping people in need and will welcome any support they can get at this time.

Recommended Online Resources

The following list of resources can also be found online on the *Survive the Great Recession* blog – www.SurviveGreatRecession.blogspot.com. The list is updated on a regular basis. Most of the sites listed are based in Ireland.

- **MABS/Money Advice and Budget Service** – www.mabs.ie. MABS is a national, free, confidential and independent service for people in debt or in danger of getting into debt. A valuable resource.

- **It'sYourMoney.ie** – www.itsyourmoney.ie. The Financial Regulator's website. Information on financial products in plain English.

- **Citizen Information Board** – www.citizeninformationboard.ie. Offers information, advice and advocacy.

- **LosingYourJob.ie** – www.losingyourjob.ie. This website is offered by the Citizen Information Board. It provides public information for those who are currently unemployed or are becoming unemployed in Ireland.

- **County and City Enterprise Boards (CEBs)** – www.enterpriseboards.ie. CEBs provide support for small businesses with 10 employees or less, at the local level.

- **Department of Social and Family Affairs** – www.welfare.ie. Another website that is a valuable source of information.

- **FAS** – www.fas.ie. FAS is Ireland's National Training & Employment Authority.

- **Department of Enterprise, Trade and Employment** – www.entemp.ie. This website is devoted to growing Ireland's competitiveness and quality employment.

- **Teagasc** – www.teagasc.ie. This is the website of the Agriculture and Food Development Authority.

- **Health Service Executive (HSE)** – www.hse.ie. The Health Service Executive (HSE) is responsible for providing Health and Personal Social Services for everyone living in the Republic of Ireland.

- **Creditunion.ie** – www.creditunion.ie. A good place to start in learning more about credit unions.

- **First Step** – www.first-step.ie. A not-for-profit organisation which provides micro-financing.

- **Citizens Information** – www.citizensinformation.ie. This is an Irish eGovernment website provided by the Citizens Information Board. The site provides public service information for Ireland.

- **Volunteer Centres Ireland** – www.volunteer.ie. Information on volunteering in different parts of Ireland.

- **The Career Break Site** – www.thecareerbreaksite.com. Information on volunteering oversees and in the UK.

- **Inclusion Ireland** – www.inclusionireland.ie. Inclusion Ireland is a national voluntary organisation working to promote the rights of people with an intellectual disability in Ireland to ensure their full participation in society.

- **Easy Health** - www.easyhealthandliving.com. Useful information for healthy living in recessionary times.

- **The Ideas Campaign** – www.ideascampaign.com. This website solicits people's ideas for promoting economic growth during these recessionary times.

- **Green Options** – www.greenoptions.com. Green Options is a community of blogs dedicated to helping you figure out what sustainability means to you.

- **IrishJobs.ie** – www.irishjobs.ie. This is one of several sites that are available as a resource for people doing an online job search for jobs in Ireland.

- **Top Job Sites** – www.topjobsites.com. Provides information primarily on American-based job search sites.

About the Contributors

Phyllis Brennan in an advisor with the MABS office in Ballymun, North Dublin.

Christopher Condren is a self-employed heating and plumbing contractor living in North London.

Aileen Doyle is Manager of the Home Services Programme based in Ballymun, North Dublin.

Michael Deevy is an advocate for individuals with disabilities and is chairperson of the Laois Friends for Special Needs.

Linda Desmond is CEO of CARELOCAL, an agency providing services for older citizens in Dublin.

Deborah Dooley, a freelance journalist, operates the Writers Retreat in the village of Sheepwash in Devon, England.

Mary McVeigh is a teacher and mother who lives in Carbury, County Kildare. She is on leave from her job as a secondary school teacher in order to focus on raising her children.

Paddy O'Brien, a businessman and credit union volunteer, lives in Kilnamanagh, Dublin.

Katherine O'Leary writes a weekly column for the *Irish Farmers Journal.*

Lorna Roe works in the area of social policy for Age Action Ireland.

Jean Roberts has her own home-based training business located in Sligo, Ireland. She is the administrator for HANDLE® in Ireland.

Michael Roberts, who formerly managed his own company providing automation services, has been conducting research in the field of anthropology in recent years.

Gerard Scully is Senior Information Officer for Age Action Ireland.

Steve Shea is a market research consultant based in Wakefield, Massachusetts.

Amreen Singh is an undergraduate student in psychology at the National University of Ireland at Maynooth, Co Kildare.

Selected Reading List

In this section you will find a select listing of books that may serve as resources in dealing with the economic challenges we now face. The books are listed in five categories.

The Financial Meltdown

Ireland's Economic Crash: A Radical Agenda for Change (The Liffey Press, 2009) by Kieran Allen. This book recounts how a miracle economy turned into an economic disaster zone. Professor Allen challenges some of the key assumptions about the capitalist system. The kind of thought-provoking book that's really worth reading.

Who Really Runs Ireland? (Penguin Ireland, 2009) by Matt Cooper. A startling account of how the newly wealthy influenced the exercise of power in Ireland and how it led to economic catastrophe.

The Bankers (Penguin Ireland, 2009) by Shane Ross. The inside story of Ireland's banking meltdown.

Banksters (Hatchette Books 2009) by David Murphy of RTE and Martina Devlin of the *Irish Independent*. The two reporters document the story behind the meltdown of major Irish financial institutions.

Fool's Gold: How Unrestrained Greed Corrupted a Dream, Shattered Global Markets and Unleashed a Catastrophe by

Gillian Tett (Little, Brown, 2009). The inside story of the financial crisis – from a journalist who predicted it.

House of Cards: How Wall Street's Gamblers Broke Capitalism (Allen Lane, 2009) by William D. Cohan. Another book providing inside information on how the financial crash came about.

The Storm: The World Economic Crisis & What It Means by Vince Cable (Atlantic Books, 2009). Cable explains the causes of the world economic crisis and how we should respond to the challenges it brings. Highly recommended.

Coping with Redundancy

Take Charge of Your Career...and Find a Job You Really Love (The Liffey Press, 2009) by Dr. Corina Grace. This is one of the best books available for anyone considering a career change. Highly recommended.

Know Your Rights (Blackwell Publishing, 2009) by Andrew McCann. A guide to social and civic entitlements in Ireland. An invaluable source of information.

Surviving the Axe by Lisa O'Callaghan (Liberties Press, 2009). An informative book that manages to include humour on a most difficult subject. Highly recommended.

Winning Job Interviews by Dr. Paul Powers (Career Press, 2006). In this easy-to-follow book, author, psychologist, and career expert Dr. Powers shows job hunters how to find and land the job they love.

How to Safely Quit the Day Job: Retiring Early in Economically Tough Times by Ian Mitchell (Blackwell Publishing, 2009). Mixes anecdotal case studies and humour. Covers all aspects of retirement and career change.

Redundancy: A Development Opportunity for You! By Frank Scott-Lennon, Brian McIvor & Fergus Berry (Management Briefs, 2009). A valuable resource for any individual who finds themselves in a redundancy situation.

Job Shift: How to Prosper in a Workplace Without Jobs by William Bridges (Da Capo Press, 1995). This prophetic book predicated the major changes in the workplace over the past fifteen years.

How to Get a Job You'll Love (McGraw Hill, 2008) by John Lees. Information for anyone looking for a new career path.

Promoting Resilience

Creating the Resilient Organization (Prentice Hall, 1995) by Edward Deevy. A blueprint for managers on how to engage and motivate employees.

Resilience: The Power to Bounce Back When the Going Gets Tough (Hartherleigh, 1997). This book highlights how we can get stuck in our own negativity rather than turning situations around to our advantage.

Adjusting the Sails: Resilience Strategies for Professionals by M.L. Lightner (M & M Discoveries, 2000). Insights into how you can put action plans in place to help you develop more resilience.

Future Search: An Action Guide to Finding Common Ground in Communities by Marvin Weisbord & Sandra Janoff (Berrett-Koehler, 2000). This practical guide offers principles, techniques, and examples for running successful future search conferences.

Building Resiliency: How to Thrive in Times of Change by Mary Lynn Pulley and Michael Wakefield (CCL Press, 2001). This guidebook defines resiliency and describes how you can develop your own store of resiliency.

Rally the Troops: How to Get the Whole Organization Engaged with the Business (DGI, 2003) by Edward Deevy. A workbook on organisational transformation. For more information contact the author – eddeevy@cs.com

Wellness at Work: Building Resilience to Job Stress (New Harbinger Publishers, 1995) by V. O'Hara. How to build wellness into your everyday life and into the life of your organisation.

Leadership & Managing Change

Managing Transitions: Making the Most of Change, 2nd edition, by William Bridges (William Bridges & Associates, 2003). Building on his earlier book describing the three stages that people typically go through during a major change in their lives, Bridges describes how to deal with the emotional challenges of each of these stages.

Leading Change by John Kotter (Harvard Business School Press, 1996). Kotter offers a practical eight-step process for managing change in organisations.

Serious Creativity by Edward de Bono (Harper Collins, 1992). Edward de Bono is a champion of creative techniques. This book is a guide to how you can utilise your creativity to best effect.

The Empowered Manager: Positive Political Skills at Work by Peter Block (Jossey Bass, 1987). This book is a classic on how to create employee empowerment. Highly recommended for any manager or supervisor.

The Human Side of Enterprise by Douglas McGregor (1960). McGregor's Theory X-Theory Y opened up a whole new way of thinking about how to motivate employees.

The Servant as Leader by Robert K. Greenleaf (Robert K. Greenleaf Centre, 1991). An inspiring book on leadership that challenges traditional thinking on the role of the leader.

One Minute Manager by Kenneth Blanchard & Spencer Johnson (Blanchard Family Partnership, 1982). Blanchard, a former colleague from the University of Massachusetts, has written many popular bestselling management books. This is an easy to read book on a simple technique for improving employee performance.

On Becoming a Leader by Warren Bennis (Arrow, 1998). Bennis, a prolific writer of management books, explains how people become leaders.

Leadership and the New Science by Margaret Wheatley (Berrett-Koehler, 1994). Ms. Wheatley pushes our thinking about people in a new direction.

Leadership is an Art by Max DePree (Dell Publishing, 1989). My favourite book on leadership written by a CEO who really believed that his employees were his best asset.

Advice /Self-Help/Motivation

Balancing Your Life: A Practical Guide to Work, Time, Money and Happiness by Anne B. Ryan (The Liffey Press, 2002). A practical guide on how to leave the rat race behind and start living again.

Sit Tight & Get it Right: How to Beat the Recession Blues in Ireland edited by Caroline Madden & Laura Slattery (Blackhall Publishing, 2009). Experienced writers and experts from a variety of backgrounds offer advice on a wide range of subjects.

Outliers: The Story of Success by Malcolm Gladwell (Little Brown, 2008). The author looks at what makes for high levels of success and presents some interesting findings for the reader to ponder.

The Power of Now by Eckhart Tolle (Hodder & Stoughton, 1999). This practical mystic's modern gospel offers transcendent truths to set us free.

The Hungry Spirit: New Thinking for a New World by Charles Handy (Arrow, 2002). An inspiring book – sometimes provocative, always intensely personal, and ultimately full of hope.

The Seven Habits of Highly Effective People by Stephen Covey (Simon & Schuster, 1990). One of the most popular self-improvement books published in the last twenty years. Presents a holistic, integrated, principle-centred approach to solving personal and professional problems.

The Complete Guide to Stress Management by Chandra Patel (Vermilian, 1996). Looks at the causes and symptoms of stress and suggests a series of exercises and relaxation techniques which help alleviate the harmful effects of stress.

About the Author

FOR MORE THAN TWO DECADES Ed Deevy has divided his time as a management psychologist between Ireland and the United States. He has specialised in helping both for-profit and not-for-profit organisations improve employee morale and productivity. Over the past ten years he has pioneered the use of a process called *Rally the Troops*. This structured process is designed to get the whole organisation engaged in support of organisational goals.

Author of *Creating the Resilient Organization* (Prentice Hall, 1995), he has spoken internationally to business and professional groups on such topics as culture change, employee engagement and how to promote resiliency within the organisation.

Deevy holds a doctorate in Organizational Behaviour from the University of Massachusetts at Amherst. He became a licensed psychologist in the Commonwealth of Massachusetts in 1981. A native of County Laois, he currently resides in Kilnamanagh, South Dublin.

Reader Feedback is Welcome

Any thoughts you want to share with the author on the contents of this book? It's easy. Simply go to the *Survive the Great Recession* blog – www.SurviveGreatRecession.blogspot.com. Scroll down and click on 'comments'. This blog is updated regularly and has further information on the issues discussed in this book.

Additional copies of *How to Survive the Great Recession* can be purchased at your local bookstore or directly from The Liffey Press website– www.theliffeypress.com.

Dr. Deevy is available for presentations on 'Surviving the Great Recession' to organisations and groups. For more information, or to schedule a presentation, contact Jean Roberts by email at jeanroberts@eircom.net.